Understanding Other Religious Worlds

FAITH MEETS FAITH

An Orbis Series in Interreligious Dialogue
Paul F. Knitter & William R. Burrows, General Editors
Editorial Advisors
John Berthrong
Diana Eck
Karl-Josef Kuschel
Lamin Sanneh
George E. Tinker
Felix Wilfred

In the contemporary world, the many religions and spiritualities stand in need of greater communication and cooperation. More than ever before, they must speak to, learn from, and work with each other in order to maintain their vital identities and to contribute to fashioning a better world.

The FAITH MEETS FAITH Series seeks to promote interreligious dialogue by providing an open forum for exchange among followers of different religious paths. While the Series wants to encourage creative and bold responses to questions arising from contemporary appreciations of religious plurality, it also recognizes the multiplicity of basic perspectives concerning the methods and content of interreligious dialogue.

Although rooted in a Christian theological perspective, the Series does not limit itself to endorsing any single school of thought or approach. By making available to both the scholarly community and the general public works that represent a variety of religious and methodological viewpoints, FAITH MEETS FAITH seeks to foster an encounter among followers of the religions of the world on matters of common concern.

FAITH MEETS FAITH SERIES

Understanding Other Religious Worlds

A Guide for Interreligious Education

Judith A. Berling

ORBIS BOOKS

Maryknoll, New York 10545

Library of Congress Cataloging-in-Publication Data

Berling, Judith A.
    Understanding other religious worlds : a guide for interreligious
education / Judith A. Berling.
        p. cm. — (Faith meets faith)
    Includes bibliographical references and index.
    ISBN 1-57075-516-7
    1. Religions—Study and teaching. 2. Christianity and other
religions. I. Title. II. Series.
BL41 .B46 2004
261.2—dc22

                                              2003022542

Contents

Preface

The events of September 11, 2001, stunned us with a graphic reminder that religious difference and misunderstanding can be a source of unspeakable violence. This lesson has long been with us, of course—in the Balkans, in the Middle East, in Northern Ireland, in Kashmir, places where all too often religious difference has marked the "other" as enemy.[1] In the wake of September 11, some Americans tarred all Muslims for the acts of a few extreme fundamentalists. Some attacked Hindus and Sikhs, mistaking them for Muslims, whom they mistakenly assumed universally to be terrorists. In the course of human history (and even in our very young century) violence has been perpetrated in the name of religion—not just in the name of other religions but also in the name of Christianity. While the tragic destruction of September 11 brought such violence to an unprecedented level, the United States landscape has long been scarred by religious violence: vandalism against synagogues, Buddhist and Hindu temples, and African American churches. Given that sorry history, it is incumbent upon all religions to educate their members about interreligious relations, and it is incumbent upon Christians in the United States to learn about and understand other religions.

Americans have a position of prominence in the world, and Christians have a position of prominence in the United States. That position of prominence and privilege carries a responsibility. It is important that American Christians be a source of solutions, not a source of the problem—that our understanding of the world be as broad and deep as our prominence, that we exercise appropriate wisdom, modesty, and humility, both as Americans and as Christians. At the very least, our prominence in the world as Americans and in the culture as Christians invites us to extend the hand of friendship at home and abroad, expressing Christian regard for our neighbors. This book was written to help Christians learn to understand and establish good relationships with persons of other religions.

THE SEEDS OF THIS BOOK

The personal historical seeds of this book go back to 1965, when I was a junior at Carleton College considering a vocation for ministry. A startling per-

---

[1] September 11 and these other conflicts are far too complex to have been simply "caused" by religious difference. The tragedy is the way in which religious difference can so readily be claimed or exploited to deepen or perpetuate conflict.

sonal encounter with anti-Asian racism in a parish and an outstanding class on
Chinese religions convinced me that my vocation was to the classroom, specifically, to be a teacher of Asian religions, a bridge to help my fellow Americans
and my fellow Christians understand and appreciate non-Western religions and
cultures.[2] I dropped my plans for seminary and enrolled in graduate school to
study Chinese religions and cultures.

Upon graduation I took a job teaching East Asian Religions at Indiana University in Bloomington, Indiana, in the heartland of America and the Bible Belt.
When I arrived at IU in the mid-1970s, undergraduates had not yet grasped the
demographic changes caused by immigration because immigrants were not as
visible in the middle of the country as at its borders. The university students still
unquestioningly accepted the notion that theirs was a Christian nation. Those of
us who taught non-Western cultures were struggling to open young eyes and
minds to the reality that lay ahead.

While at IU, I was also regularly involved in workshops for secondary and
junior high teachers on teaching religion and/or Asian cultures in the public
schools. This work with public school teachers challenged my professorial stub-
bornness about "covering the material" to cut through to the most basic issues
and consider and develop effective teaching strategies that could nurture cross-
cultural and interreligious understanding.

After twelve years in a large state university where we were enjoined to "teach
about religion," but never to "teach religion," I surprised myself and my colleagues by moving to theological education as Dean and Vice President of the
Graduate Theological Union in Berkeley, a consortium of five Protestant and
three Roman Catholic seminaries, and a Unitarian Universalist school for the
ministry. The GTU also has a number of centers and affiliates, including Buddhist, Eastern Orthodox, and Jewish institutes. At the GTU, the study of religion
was admittedly religious; scholars took the religious claims of others seriously
and brought their own religious perspectives and locations to their studies. There
was a hard and lively critical edge to scholarship and teaching at the GTU, but it
came more from the interaction of multiple religious perspectives than from any
claim to objective study of religion. The plurality of perspectives was intensified
by the demographic diversity of the Bay Area.

My move to the GTU was a significant clarification of, or a return to, my
vocation. At Indiana, my job was to teach and interpret Chinese culture as part of
the general education of the college student. At the GTU, my job was to bring an
authentic voice of Chinese religions and cultures to theological education and to
the ecumenical/interfaith conversation of the consortium. The move to theological education thus had at least two dimensions of impact on my role as
teacher/scholar. First, in terms of my role in the classroom, I was now less the
authoritative interpreter of Chinese culture (the cultural bridge between East and

---

[2] My encounter with racism and the impact of the course are discussed in more detail in Judith
A. Berling, *A Pilgrim in Chinese Culture: Negotiating Religious Diversity* (Maryknoll, N.Y.: Orbis
Books, 1997), 6-8.

West) than a reporter of Asian views or a facilitator of a cross-cultural and inter-religious conversation. It was not my job to construct the authoritative narrative of Chinese religion so much as to bring in authentic voices and issues from Chinese religious traditions and to facilitate a conversation between those voices and other traditions. This new classroom role was underscored by the shift in student population: my classroom now included, alongside Christians and Jews who knew little of Asian religions or cultures, Buddhists and Daoists as well as Christians of Asian descent and Americans who had lived extensively in Asia.

Second, I found myself in a new institutional role as a scholar of Chinese religions. My background in Asian religions was welcomed as an asset for the GTU, but it was far from clear how to contribute to the general education of the theological students. The growing number of requirements imposed by the seminary curricula and denominations left little room for electives, so only a tiny percentage of students would take a separate course on another religion. Moreover, attempts to bring other religious perspectives into core courses were constrained by time, by the way the Christian agendas of the courses defined and delimited the issues, and by the lack of background on the part of professors. Along with the small handful of faculty trained in Asian religions, I have struggled at the GTU to discern the most realistic and effective way to bring the perspectives of Asian religions into the theological education of M.Div. students.

After years of discussing these issues in the same way and making little headway, I gradually began to realize that if I were to draw on all aspects of my background I might be able to offer a fresh approach to conversation that might move past at least some of the old obstacles. I bring to this book my dual backgrounds as a scholar of East Asian religions and as a student of teaching and learning theory to promote a conversation about how theological students (and Christians) *learn* other religions.

NATURE AND AUDIENCE OF THE BOOK

This is a different conversation than the several that theological schools have had over the past decades. It bypasses the theological issues of exclusivist ecclesiologies and christologies, or any attempt to formulate a "wider ecumenism" or "theology of religions." Such issues are significant and challenging, but they will not be resolved quickly and can perhaps be more effectively resolved if and when Christians—including theologians—become more knowledgeable about other religions. At that point some of those issues may drop away as irrelevant; others will be clarified. It also bypasses specific content: *what* we should teach about other religions. The "content" issues must be addressed in terms of specific institutional/denominational situations and relationships; efforts to address interreligious teaching become stalled when we seek to determine the content before understanding the basic nature of the enterprise. In this book I step back and look at some prior issues about what is entailed in learning other religions.

This book is written to stimulate reflection, conversation, and new ideas among colleagues in theological education (both faculty and students), persons in pastoral and lay leadership in the churches, and thoughtful fellow Christians who are concerned about understanding and establishing relationships with persons of other faiths. I do not come to the project thinking that I have all the answers, but I do come with a particular point of view.

The learning theories I discuss in this book (1) emphasize understanding, as opposed to the simple inculcation of information; (2) argue that knowledge is constructed through human conversation, rather than simply being "out there" to be discovered or memorized; and (3) propose conversational approaches to learning that encourage students to speak from their own experiences and to hear and understand others across the lines of difference, rather than theories that offer a monocultural perspective on "objective" knowledge. In turning to these sorts of learning theories, I do not intend to deny that there are claims to be made for other, more traditional theories. As one who studied Chinese and Japanese in graduate school, I have invested years of my life in rote memorization of characters, vocabulary, grammar, and sentence patterns. Until I had absorbed this information, understanding the languages was impossible. I also learned a great deal of information about the history and development of Chinese and Japanese cultures. Without this factual background, I would have had no context for understanding specific issues. I realize that higher education, both theological and secular, is to a large extent committed to "traditioning" students into certain communities of discourse—whether the community of United Methodists or the community of American historians. Nonetheless, the learning theories I discuss in this book are important precisely because they have emerged as a corrective to and qualification of entrenched habits of teaching and learning that are not adequate for education in a diverse world. These are the theories from which I have benefited as a teacher engaging increasingly diverse classrooms; they have challenged me to think hard about learning, and hence about teaching. I am writing in the hope that these ideas will stir new thoughts in my readers.

I am also acutely aware that not all Christians share my assumptions about the importance of Christian responses to religious pluralism. The legacy of Christian exclusivism is deeply rooted in Christian history and has become intertwined with issues that in the minds of many are key to Christian identity. I certainly respect the sincerity and depth of those convictions among fellow Christians. I invite them to read this book, but acknowledge that many will not be open to or ready for all of its ideas. However, I hope that the book may provide some small openings for such readers to consider what sorts of understanding of other religions may be possible.

This book is addressed to Christians who are wrestling with the relationship of Christianity to other religions, Christians who find it hard to accept that God is not somehow at work in the lives of sincere Buddhists, Hindus, and others. Christians who want to be more open to other religions are struggling with how they can justify this in theological terms. This book offers them another route—a route to understanding other religions. It argues that such learning leads to new relationships and new self-understandings within the Christian communities that might, over time, create a sounder foundation for developing a theological under-standing of Christian relationships with other religions.

The book's intended audience is primarily theological scholars (faculty and students), church leaders, and thoughtful Christians. However, I would not be very serious about religious pluralism if I were not also concerned about how Jews, Buddhists, Muslims, Hindus, and so on learn other religions as well. I have written from what I know, which is Christian theological education. I invite col-leagues from other religious communities to read the work and consider what changes would be required to adapt the ideas to their own communities. What, for instance, are their traditions of and current issues about "religious learning"? Are there assumptions about dealing with people of other religions, about the sources of religious knowledge, or about the religious purposes of learning that would significantly shape their approaches to learning other religions?

Finally, although this book focuses on theological learning, I am also deeply concerned with the teaching of religious studies in this society. A good deal of the book is pertinent to religious studies, if one makes the assumption (as I do) that perhaps the major cultural role for religious studies is to create the basis for understanding and relationships across lines of difference in our pluralistic soci-ety. However, the public discourse about religion in our culture is still fraught with confusion and misunderstanding. To address the issues of religious studies would require a different sort of book.

ACKNOWLEDGMENTS

This book would not have been possible without the help and support of many parties. I am grateful to the Association of Theological Schools and the Henry Luce Foundation for naming me a Henry Luce III Fellow in Theology. This fel-lowship gave me a full year's sabbatical to research and write this book, and that made all the difference. I am grateful to the Graduate Theological Union for my sabbatical leave and for generous support all along the way. I am grateful to col-leagues John Berthrong, James Bretzke, Kathryn Campbell, Sheila Chan-drasekhar, Bill Countryman, Sue Diehl, Clare Fischer, Geoffrey Foy, Matthew Haar Farris, Kathleen Kook, Maureen Maloney, Fumitaka Matsuoka, Alda Mor-gan, Norrie Palmer, Richard Payne, Patricia Shannon, Kathleen Talvacchia, Denis Thalson, Kimberly Whitney, Philip Wickeri, and Raymond Williams, who read this book in draft form, offering their criticisms, suggestions, and their own experiences. Finally, I am grateful to my friend and partner Rhoda Bunnell, who offered her support and encouragement in every possible way from the beginning to the end of the process.

Introduction

Chapter 1 opens the book with a discussion of Christians and religious diversity. It explores how U.S. society has come to be so religiously diverse, and the challenges this diversity poses for Christians. This chapter articulates my theological premises, but lays no claim to having addressed or solved all the theological issues of Christians and other religions. I do not seek to resolve those issues in the book, but to aid Christians in learning other religions. Understanding other religions, I argue, can forge a foundation from which, in the long run, the difficult theological issues may be addressed.

The next section of the book (chapters 2 through 4) explores ideas and issues in three distinct but related fields—learning theory, study of other religions, and theological learning. Many faculty colleagues shy away from learning theory, believing it to be of dubious value, best relegated to the specialists in education. Too many faculty and students rush directly toward engaging subject matter without any critical reflection on the processes, purposes, and issues of teaching and learning. Teaching consumes a great deal of the time and energy of faculty, and learning of students, and yet many think teaching and learning can be ignored in favor of focusing solely on the subject matter at hand. While I share a passion for the subject matter, my experience as a teacher has taught me again and again that the subject matter does not simply teach itself. I have to understand my students, the backgrounds and learning goals that they bring to the classroom, and how best to help them achieve appropriate goals. Learning theory has helped me to understand and evaluate my students and the learning process so that I can be more effective as a teacher. I urge my readers to set aside whatever aversion they may have to learning theory and engage the learning theorists in chapter 2, as their ideas work together with those in chapters 3 and 4 to provide the theoretical background of the learning process that is the heart of this book.

Each of the three disciplines contributes substantially to the articulation of the learning process. Teaching and learning theory addresses the issues of learning within a diverse world, coming to understand and negotiate areas of human difference. The study of religions addresses issues in understanding religious difference, particularly in light of recent critiques of Western approaches to the study of religious others. Theological learning addresses particular issues for Christians, particularly the need to balance between the appropriation of tradition and its reappropriation in light of changing circumstances.

Building on those three disciplines, I articulate in chapter 5 the threads of a process for Christians learning another religion, unpacking some of the elements involved in that process so that each can be examined carefully in its own right.

There is a tendency, when we think about learning or teaching another religion, to focus almost entirely on one of these threads, to have a dominant concern or worry. While that is perfectly understandable, it has the unfortunate effect of obscuring other dimensions of the learning process, so that most approaches to learning other religions are skewed in one direction or another. While perfect balance is a utopian ideal, the unraveling of the threads of the learning process helps to evaluate the effectiveness of various approaches, whether in the classroom or beyond. Without such awareness, it will not be possible to improve or refine the ways in which Christians learn other religions.

Unraveling, naming, and describing the threads of the learning process offer an interpretation of that process. The five threads are (1) encountering difference or entering another world; (2) one's initial response as a Christian; (3) conversation and dialogue on several levels; (4) living out what has been learned; and (5) internalizing the learning process. Many other interpretations are possible, and some may well turn out to be more useful or productive than what is offered in this book. If the threads of the learning process are suggested as an interpretation of the learning process—a particular reading of it—they are not offered as an "objective" structure or model. The articulation of these various threads is a device to bring to light several facets of what is admittedly a complex process. Its purpose is to develop a particular form of awareness, an alertness to dimensions of learning that may be overlooked, to the detriment of the learner and, ultimately, of the communities in which the learner participates. They are intended to serve as well-written program notes that enable the audience to hear nuances in a work of music or see dimensions of a dance or play they might otherwise miss.

The last section of the book (chapters 6 and 7) turns to the practical aspects of teaching and learning other religions. Based on the learning process articulated in chapter 5 and conversations with fellow teachers, chapter 6 critiques and assesses common classroom strategies and suggests ways of enhancing the process of learning other religions. Chapter 7 moves beyond the classroom to talk about learning in less formal church settings, providing practical guidelines for making the most of such learning experiences. Appendix A provides an annotated bibliography for teaching other religions, and Appendix B offers a checklist of Practical Guidelines for Christians Learning Other Religions.

Nonacademic readers may want to begin with chapter 1 and then move directly to the practical chapters (6 and 7) before returning to chapter 5, which discusses the learning process in more depth. They may then consult chapters 2 through 4 as they are relevant and helpful. Throughout the book I have sought to address both the academic and the broader audience, but chapters 2 through 4 may be a bit "heady" for some nonacademics.

The book contains some deliberate repetition; I circle back to earlier points to clarify how each chapter has built upon earlier ideas. Some readers may not need the repetition; if so, I invite them to skim over these sections and pick up where the discussion moves forward. Other readers will find these sections helpful, seeing ever more clearly how the ideas of the various authors cited are woven together into the threads of the learning process, which in turns helps illumine various approaches to learning other religions.

WHY MAKE THE EFFORT
TO LEARN OTHER RELIGIONS?

In one way this book is behind its time, since religious diversity has been an increasing fact of the lives of U.S. Christians for decades. In some parts of the country, the inability of Christians to help parishioners deal with the religious diversity of their lives, their workplaces, and their families has driven people from the churches; it is simpler to be "spiritual, but not religious" than to wrestle with the complications of maintaining Christian faith in a religiously diverse world.

In another way, this book is ahead of its time, for theological schools and congregations are still uncomfortable with and resistant to addressing the presence of other religions. There are understandable reasons for this. In the churches and in the theological schools, many Christians feel that they have at best a tenuous grasp of their own heritage, that their primary need is to learn the Christian tradition. The issue of other religions seems a distraction from that task. This book does not argue against the desire for a deeper grounding in Christian traditions, discussion, and issues. It does, however, reject the premise that one must choose between the two. Just as learning another language deepens my understanding of English, and just as coming to know other persons helps me understand myself, so learning other religions brings my Christianity into sharper relief and helps me notice and own what I earlier took for granted.

Second, if they are to confront other religions at all, many would prefer a succinct authoritative summary of the sort offered in the traditional course on the world's religions. We are impatient; we want our information clear and neatly packaged so that we can take it in and get on with life. We also seek a clear structure or framework on which to rest so that we feel sure of our footing; prepackaged summaries seem to provide that. We don't like the discomfort of being stretched beyond the familiar, with its unknown consequences. Such indeed is the easier way, but to follow the easier way is to withdraw from genuine engagement with the voices of other religions and to pull back into an increasingly inward-looking, isolated, and atrophied church.

If the lives of Christians are to be increasingly marked by religious diversity in the workplace, the schools, and the family; if U.S. society is to become increasingly religiously diverse; if there is to be any hope that American Christians can provide leadership for the world to move beyond religious intolerance and violence, then Christians must begin to understand and engage other religions as part of their Christian lives and understanding. Learning other religions is a requirement for living as Christians in a religiously diverse world.

1

Christians and Religious Diversity

THE COLOR-CODED MAP

I remember as a young schoolgirl studying textbooks introducing the world's religions using a color-coded map of the world. The pink tones of "Hinduism" colored India and parts of Indonesia and Sri Lanka. The yellow tones of Buddhism colored East and Southeast Asia. The blue tones of Islam colored Pakistan, parts of Indonesia, and most of the Arab world and North Africa. The purple tones of Christianity colored North and South America and Europe. The map included codes for "indigenous" religions in Africa, "outback" Australia, Papua New Guinea, and a few other "remote" cultures. Each religion had its territory and its cultural home; the world was divided into religious enclaves, and religions other than Christianity were spatially and culturally removed from my world.

Moreover, the religion texts of my youth taught the origins of the world religions, the stories of "the founders." Conforming to a Protestant sensibility of seeing "true" religious teaching as associated with "the teachings of the founder," "true" Buddhism was defined as the teachings of the historical Buddha, and "true" Islam was associated with the life and teachings of Muhammad. The emphasis on origins removed these traditions from my life not only in space but in time. I was only vaguely conscious of the presence of Buddhists, Hindus, and Muslims in the contemporary world; and, when brought to an awareness of them, I was startled when what I saw and heard of contemporary practices did not conform to the depiction of "true" religion in my textbooks.

Over the past thirty-five years, scholars of religion have come to realize that the depictions in such textbooks were an oversimplified and romantic construction of Euroamerican views of the religious world. The texts all too conveniently removed the "other religions" to a safe distance, spatially, temporally, and culturally; they rendered them exotic "others." Ironically, the texts sometimes created a "religion" where the adherents had seen no unity, only a plethora of diverse traditions. "Hinduism," for example, was the invention of European scholars, not of "Hindus."[1] As Edward Said famously argued, Europeans invented "the Orient" and "orientalism" as an "other" against which they could define their own identity.[2]

The color-coded religious map of the world was, even in its heyday, a romantic projection. However, subsequent events destroyed any vestiges of its credibility. The forces of immigration and globalization have broken up the large color blocks, as in a giant kaleidoscope, into tiny fragments of colors scattered through virtually all corners of the globe.

The "other religions" (various forms of Hinduism, Buddhism, Islam, Jainism, and indigenous traditions) are well established in Europe and North America, while Christianity has a distinctly global presence. In my own Anglican communion (which has long seen itself as centered in the "motherland" of the United Kingdom), the demographic center of the church has moved to Africa. This shift is challenging Euroamerican notions about who dominates and defines the Anglican communion. Issues of biblical interpretation and church doctrine raised by African and Asian Anglicans at the 1998 Lambeth Conference challenged more "liberal" views of many American and European Anglicans.

The global movement of peoples of all traditions has in many ways challenged unitary views of the world religions. The various "religions" are now adapting to a variety of cultures around the globe, embracing or resisting the forces of modernization, and testing their identification with their "traditional" cultures of origin. American-born Zen Buddhists are conflicted about whether to accept all of the Japanese cultural traditions associated with Zen. Muslims and Sikhs in the United States are conflicted about whether to observe dress codes and customs that would be mandatory in their cultures of origin. Africans and Chinese are creating "new" Christianities strongly "spiced" with their own traditional cultural practices and sensibilities.

The once "remote" religions of my student textbooks now surround me, not simply as institutions (temples, mosques, meditation centers, gurdwaras) but also as people with whom I meet and interact on a daily basis—in schools, in the marketplace, in hospitals, at work, and even in my church. Sikhs drive most of the taxicabs in Berkeley. The X-ray technician who took numerous chest films when I had pneumonia was a Muslim. The admissions officer at my school is a Hindu. My local Episcopal church includes a dozen parishioners in interfaith marriages; several more who have children or siblings who are practicing other faiths; an ordained deacon who spent thirty years of her life as a Hindu; and an active member who practices intensive Buddhist meditation alongside his Christian disciplines. A score of other parishioners have roots in Asian or African cultures and thus bring religious and ethical influences with them from their pasts. It is abundantly clear that I no longer live in the religiously color-coded world of my school textbooks.

---

[1] See Richard King, *Orientalism and Religion: Postcolonial Theory, India, and 'The Mystic East'* (London/New York: Routledge, 1999), chapter 5, "The Myth of 'Hinduism,'" 96–117.

[2] Edward Said, *Orientalism* (New York: Vintage Books, 1979).

One example sums up the change very nicely. In 1893 the World's Parliament of Religions was held in Chicago in conjunction with the World's Fair. This gathering brought leaders of many religions from all over the globe, many of them the first public representatives of these traditions on North American soil. When the planning began for the 1993 centennial of the Parliament, the leaders realized that the religions present at the 1893 parliament now had representatives within easy distance of virtually every major urban center in the United States. The "world's religions" are among us.[3]

HOW DID RELIGIOUS DIVERSITY OVERTAKE THE COLOR-CODED MAP?

Even during my school days, the color-coded map of the world's religions glossed over religious diversity in the United States. The traditions of Native Americans had long predated the coming of Christianity, but before the 1970s the general public was largely ignorant of these traditions. The publication of *Black Elk Speaks* and the work of native scholars such as Vine Deloria had not brought knowledge of these traditions to the attention of the reading public.[4] Chinese immigrants to the West Coast, working on railroads, in mines, or as servants and cooks, had brought with them Buddhist, Confucian, and Daoist practices, but these were not widely known or acknowledged and were often suppressed. Other immigrants brought with them Hindu, Buddhist, or Muslim practices, but their small numbers were sufficiently scattered that they were not a visible presence. In 1955, Will Herberg published an influential study of the sociology of religion in the United States, entitled *Protestant, Catholic, Jew.*[5] At that time, not only were these the dominant and visible religions but, as Herberg demonstrated, the religions that influenced the structures and voting patterns of American life. Herberg's book ignored the long-standing presence of Buddhists and other Asian religions, particularly in the American West, and a host of native and immigrant traditions that were still largely invisible to the wider public or expected to disappear as adherents were assimilated to mainstream culture.

The 1965 Immigration and Naturalization Act began to erode that invisibility. The act ended highly restrictive immigration policies targeted against Asians in particular, opening the doors to new immigrants who brought with them their cultures, languages, cuisines, and religions.

The flow of immigration from Asia and the Pacific to North America was per-

---

[3] For instance, at California State University at Hayward, students in the courses on world religions regularly include adherents of five of the six religions taught in the course (Patricia Shannon, personal communication, June 6, 2002).

[4] *Black Elk Speaks; Being the Life Story of a Holy Man of the Oglala Sioux as Told through John G. Neihardt* (Lincoln: University of Nebraska Press, 1979). See the influential work of Vine Deloria, *God is Red* (New York: Dell, 1973).

[5] Will Herberg, *Protestant, Catholic, Jew: An Essay in American Religious Sociology* (Garden City, N.Y.: Doubleday, 1955).

haps one of the first signs of globalization, a trend that gathered force during the last quarter of the twentieth century and continues into this one. Globalization is the confluence of several factors: developments in communications that "shrank" the world by putting every corner of the globe into virtually instantaneous contact with every other corner; the development of an interconnected world economy dominated by transnational corporations, which began to erode the significance of national borders and created worldwide markets for both labor and products; movements of people across national borders, largely in response to opportunities and pressures in the global marketplace; and local adaptations of or resistance to global forces. These movements of people across borders, both voluntary and involuntary, have often created a sense of displacement, a loss of place. Globalization has meant, on the one hand, that one is likely to see a young person in a Burmese village wearing Reebok shoes, a T-shirt with a picture of Michael Jordan, and a Swatch watch while drinking Coca Cola; on the other hand, globalization has meant that the cuisines, dress, arts, and citizens of cultures across the globe are now present across the United States, although the exact "mix" and pattern of global diversity vary from city to city, region to region.

Americans are aware of many issues raised by "globalization" for their communities and their cultures. Small U.S. cities have experienced and benefited from the construction of Japanese factories with Japanese management that have changed (and often revived) their local economies. Other cities are aware that their industries (such as the steel and textile industries) have fallen prey to cheaper labor, more modern plants, or government subsidies abroad. Many Americans are exploring cuisines cooked by their immigrant neighbors; they have moved on from Chinese and Japanese dishes to Thai, Vietnamese, Middle Eastern, Indian, South and Central American, Caribbean, and Ethiopian foods. Public school systems are struggling to meet the needs of children whose first language is not English, as demonstrated by the kindergarten class in Richmond, California, that includes students speaking fifteen different languages. Moreover, immigration has become a volatile political issue—illegal immigration, to be sure—but also the importation of highly trained technical workers from around the globe. In our awareness of the effects of globalization, however, there is a significant lacuna, aptly identified by Diana Eck:

> For all this discussion about immigration, language, and culture, we Americans have not yet really thought about it in terms of religion. We are surprised to discover the religious changes America has been undergoing. We are surprised to find that there are more Muslim Americans than Episcopalians, more Muslims than members of the Presbyterian Church USA, and as many Muslims as there are Jews—that is, about six million. We are astonished to learn that Los Angeles is the most complex Buddhist city in the world, with a Buddhist population spanning the whole range of the Asian Buddhist world from Sri Lanka to Korea, along with a multitude of native-born American Buddhists. . . . We know that many of our internists,

surgeons, and nurses are of Indian origin, but we have not stopped to consider that they too have a religious life, . . . that they might bring fruits and flowers to the local Shiva-Vishnu temple on the weekend and be part of a diverse Hindu population of more than a million.[6]

Eck goes on to note that living in a global society would seem to require a much greater awareness of other religions.

We cannot live in a world in which our economies and markets are global, our political awareness is global, our business relationships take us to every continent, and the Internet connects us with colleagues half a world away and yet live on Friday, or Saturday, or Sunday with ideas of God that are essentially provincial, imagining that somehow the one we call God has been primarily concerned with us and our tribe.[7]

Diana Eck's book *A New Religious America* narrates the development of the extraordinarily rich religious diversity of our society and also the ongoing struggle of all of us (Christian and non-Christian) to learn to deal with this new reality.

A NEW RELIGIOUS AMERICA

The backbone of this tale is the Immigration and Naturalization Act of 1965. The immigrants under this law continued their cultural practices, spoke their native languages, and practiced their religions in what were at first tiny and fragmented communities. They might meet in a home, a storefront, or a rented room, virtually invisible to the community around them. However, as immigrants settled in greater numbers, became economically secure, and had children, each distinct community grew concerned that its culture, language, and religious practice be handed on to succeeding generations. In the 1980s and 1990s, many groups built their own places of worship, hired religious leaders to enhance their worship and educate their children, and established a full range of cultural, linguistic, and religious programs to maintain their distinctive cultural and religious heritages.

These new immigrants came in greater numbers than ever before; they were able to avoid extreme isolation and thus to resist pressures to assimilate into mainstream culture by giving up their languages, their cultural ways, and their religious practices. They could maintain their distinctive cultural and religious roots in this country, while at the same time establishing their place in the broader mosaic of American society through work and community involvement.

---

[6] Diana L. Eck, *A New Religious America: How a "Christian Country" Has Become the World's Most Religiously Diverse Nation* (San Francisco: HarperSanFrancisco, 2001), 2-3.

[7] Ibid., 24.

The establishment of Hindu, Buddhist, or Muslim communities in the United States often requires considerable adjustment and adaptation on the part of the community. In India, for instance, Hindu temples are local, each representing a god or tradition quite distinct to the region in which the temple is established. In the United States, it is often the case that, while there are sufficient Hindus in an area to support a Hindu temple, immigrants hail from many parts of India and thus worship different Hindu gods and goddesses. In the United States, the compromise, which would seem strange indeed on Indian soil, is to honor more than one god in a particular temple, such as the temple of Shiva and Vishnu in Livermore, California. In India, Shiva and Vishnu represent quite distinct and different strands of Hindu piety.[8] Likewise, while Islam is to a certain degree united by the centrality of the Qurʾan and Qurʾanic Arabic as well as the obligations for prayer five times a day and fasting during the month of Ramadan, Islam has adapted itself to a variety of cultures as it spread across North Africa, the Near East, and Asia. The cultural differences within Islam are skillfully documented in Clifford Geertz's *Islam Observed*.[9] American Muslims establishing mosques and prayer spaces in the workplace often find themselves literally shoulder to shoulder in prayer with Muslims from throughout the world. Only the Hajj, the great pilgrimage to Mecca, offers a comparable diversity of the tradition of Islam. Buddhists have tended to cluster in temples of their own subtraditions, each speaking the language of their form of Buddhism. However, since the entire Buddhist world is represented in Los Angeles, a number of significant Pan-Buddhist organizations have developed to help Buddhists deal with their issues in representing themselves to the wider culture and to other religions in the United States.

These religious communities are also forced to adapt to American ways and styles as their young people are assimilated into U.S. culture. Thus groups have adapted Mormon-style curricula for religious education, family camps for the study of Vedanta (Hindus)[10] or for meditation (Buddhists). They establish youth choirs and youth activity groups as well as schools to teach the young people traditional languages and religious texts. These religious communities maintain the culture and religious identity of the immigrants, but they also are the means by which these traditions are recontextualized into American culture.

The increasingly visible presence and efflorescence of these non-Christian religious institutions has not come without resistance. When Buddhists, Sikhs, Jains, Hindus, and Muslims were meeting in homes or storefronts, they did not draw the attention of their neighbors, but the building of temples was another matter. For instance, Buddhist Hsi Lai Temple in Hacienda Heights, outside of Los Angeles, is a stunning complex built on fourteen acres of land. Its member-

---

[8] Ibid., 84-85. See also Norris Worrell Palmer, "Pluralism and Religious Identity: The Local Construction and Negotiation of Hindu Identity in the Face of Local and Translocal Forces" (Ph.D. diss., Graduate Theological Union, 2002).

[9] Clifford Geertz, *Islam Observed: Religious Development in Morocco and Indonesia* (New Haven: Yale University Press, 1968).

[10] Eck, *New Religious America,* 134-39.

ship is more than twenty thousand, mostly Chinese immigrants from Taiwan. The proposal to build this temple gave rise to fierce resistance from its neighbors, who sought to defeat it by means of the zoning laws. It took five years and scores of meetings to negotiate clearances. After the building was completed, the Buddhists set out to build bridges with their neighbors by distributing food baskets to the needy on Thanksgiving and Christmas and offering invitations to the entire community for dinner at the temple on major Buddhist feast days. They also invited outside groups to use their conference facilities.[11] These bridge-building activities illustrate the ways in which Buddhists and others accommodate to American religious and cultural sensibilities, as well as learn the laws and regulations governing religious organizations in American society. Hospitality to outsiders and honoring their festivals (Thanksgiving and Christmas) replicates a long-standing Chinese strategy for living with religious neighbors: participating in neighbors' feasts and then hosting the neighbors on one's own feast days as a gesture both of friendship and of gentle education about the nature and virtues of their religious community.[12] This traditional Chinese strategy has served the Hsi Lai Temple well in establishing better relationships with its Christian, Jewish, and secular neighbors.

Resistance to Hindu, Muslim, Sikh, and Buddhist religious groups sometimes takes uglier forms than fights over zoning clearances. The places of worship of these religious communities or persons with religiously distinctive dress (the dot of the Hindu woman, the turban of the Sikh man, the head scarf of the Muslim woman) have drawn the violence and hatred of some segments of society who are threatened by the presence of an "other." Because of this xenophobic violence, underscored by the events of September 11, 2001, understanding America's religious diversity and getting to know our religious neighbors is not merely a desideratum to be sought if we have the time and interest. Ignorance and misunderstanding are sources of tension and violence that have the potential to rend the fabric of an increasingly diverse U.S. society. The only alternative is mutual knowledge and understanding.

A CHALLENGE FOR CHRISTIANS

We are gradually becoming aware of the presence and proximity of numerous religions, but many Christians in the United States have not yet grasped that their religious communities are part of the totality of religions in the world, nor are we as yet aware of the place of other religions in world history. We are only beginning to realize that religious diversity is an integral part of our lives. This is so despite the fact that both biblical history and church history are rife with the ways

---

[11] Ibid., 144-48.
[12] See Judith A. Berling, *A Pilgrim in Chinese Culture: Negotiating Religious Diversity* (Maryknoll, N.Y.: Orbis Books, 1997), especially chapter 8.

in which the presence of other religions have influenced the evolution of Christian communities.

Awareness of the fact of religious diversity has not always led to an understanding or celebration of it. Christians often have a hard time accepting the reality of religious diversity or establishing appropriate relationships with religious neighbors. Their difficulties have deep historical and cultural roots.

One reason Christians have difficulties with the presence of other religions is the long history of Christian exclusivism. The insistence that Jesus Christ is the only gateway to salvation ("I am the way, and the truth, and the life; no one comes to the Father, but by me" [John 14:6]) or proclaiming *extra ecclesia nulla salus* ("outside the church there is no salvation")[13] may have helped the fragile, fledgling community of the church establish itself in its early days of persecution, but the claims of exclusivism took on an entirely different timbre as Christianity became the official church of the Holy Roman Empire and other states throughout Europe. In the course of history, Christian claims of exclusivism have too often been understood to mean that adherents of other faiths (and sometimes of other forms of Christianity) were beyond the reach of salvation. Those who affirm a triumphalist Christian exclusivism have no reason to establish relationships with persons of other faiths, except perhaps to convert them. While the Roman Catholic and formerly mainline Protestant churches have worked since the middle of the twentieth century to modify and mollify their exclusivist claims by recognizing God's presence in the lives of adherents of other religions, Christians of all stripes still struggle with the issues of exclusivism. A number of theologians, Protestant and Roman Catholic, have been wrestling with these issues over the past few decades,[14] but there are as yet no widely agreed upon answers to the questions. Nearly two thousand years of exclusivistic thinking and habits are not easy to transcend; nor are all Christians ready to transcend them. As theologians have pointed out, all too often the "solutions" to Christian exclusivism raise a host of other problems, including either a vicious relativism or a bland "all religions are equal," which actually subordinates all particular teachings to some principle or ideal that belongs to none of the traditions or that turns out to be sim-

---

[13] The Christ-centered formulation is Protestant, while the church-centered formulation is Roman Catholic.

[14] These struggles have produced a voluminous literature. See, for instance, John Hick, *An Interpretation of Religion: Human Responses to the Transcendent* (New Haven: Yale University Press, 1989); idem, *A Christian Theology of Religions: The Rainbow of Faiths* (Louisville: Westminster John Knox Press, 1995); Paul F. Knitter, *No Other Name? A Critical Survey of Christian Attitudes Toward the World Religions* (Maryknoll, N.Y.: Orbis Books, 1984); idem, *One Earth: Many Religions? Multifaith Dialogue and Global Responsibility* (Maryknoll, N.Y.: Orbis Books, 1995); idem, *Jesus and the Other Names: Christian Mission and Global Responsibility* (Maryknoll, N.Y.: Orbis Books, 1996); John Hick and Paul F. Knitter, eds., *The Myth of Christian Uniqueness* (Maryknoll, N.Y.: Orbis Books, 1987); Peter Phan, ed., *Christianity and the Wider Ecumenism* (New York: Paragon, 1990); Gavin D'Costa, ed., *Christian Uniqueness Reconsidered: The Myth of a Pluralistic Theology of Religions* (Maryknoll, N.Y.: Orbis Books, 1995); Leonard J. Swidler, *After the Absolute: The Dialogical Future of Religious Reflection* (Minneapolis: Fortress Press, 1990).

ply a restatement of Christian views of the nature of religion.[15] Christian thinkers will continue to debate these issues and look for articulations of an appropriate openness to other religions that do not undermine central Christian values.

Christian exclusivism is also related to the fact that allegiance to Christianity presents itself as a choice that entails renouncing all other religious options. Christians who hold strongly to this view are concerned that engaging another religion might be disloyal or might even lead to conversion to the other faith.

It is certainly true that learning other religions, engaging in conversation with their texts and adherents, changes one. One cannot engage in a genuine conversation without opening oneself to the views of the other; a conversation entails both mutual influence and mutual criticism. Relationships and conversations broaden one's horizons. As a result, one must reexamine and reappropriate former views and ideas, so that one's Christian identity is refined and broadened. Such interreligious conversations and influences, both friendly and competitive, have peppered the history of Christian communities. Christian doctrines have been refined and practices have been influenced and enriched by such interactions. Conversion is always a possibility, but only when there are reasons or circumstances that would lead an individual to move from one community to another. The vast majority of Christian interreligious conversations lead not to conversion but to broadened sensibilities and a clearer, if refined, sense of one's Christian identity.

There are two components to the anxiety about conversion. First, what does it mean to "join" or "convert to" another religion? Some religions actively proselytize, seeking new adherents. In such cases, outsiders are invited to make vows, sign registers, undergo initiations, or declare allegiance to a deity or teacher. Others, including many Buddhists, welcome outsiders to participate in their temples, public rituals, and practices without asking for any formal religious commitment. One could practice many forms of Buddhism rather extensively without ever "joining" the religion or renouncing one's affiliation with another religion. Second, what does it mean to "leave" one's own religion, such as Christianity? Each tradition, denomination, and movement within Christianity has its own definition about what is required to remain a faithful member. However, what is unacceptable in one form of Christianity may not be so in another. Stepping beyond the bounds of a particular denomination does not necessarily mean "leaving Christianity." Before conversion might happen, a Christian would cross at least two layers of "influence" (and each of these layers has many levels). In the first, a Christian may be influenced by the ideas or practices of another religion and may see these as enriching her Christian life and faith, with no intention of "moving to" the other community. In the second, a Christian may find herself influenced by another religion in ways that pull her beyond the accepted boundaries of her initial denomination or church, and she may subsequently seek a more open form

---

[15] S. Mark Heim, *Salvations: Truth and Difference in Religion* (Maryknoll, N.Y.: Orbis Books, 1995).

of Christianity tolerant of these new ideas or practices. Only in rare cases is the Christian so powerfully affected by the new ideas and practices that she decides to leave the Christian community entirely and "join" and exclusively practice the other religion.

In the contemporary world, many people have complex identities because of movements across cultural borders, cultural choices, racial heritage, or intermarriages. One may come from a multireligious household that seeks to honor two or more traditions. Asian American or Asian Christians can have parents or grandparents and other family members who still practice Buddhism, Confucianism, or Hinduism. Such persons often seek to honor and understand the traditions of their ancestors, which have shaped them in important ways, in harmony with their Christian identity and practices. In these cases, the "conversion" (to Christianity) took place in recent history, but the traditions of ancestors are part of the familial "cumulative tradition." What is at stake is not conversion —leaving Christianity to return to ancestral religions—but contextualization, a reconciliation of cultural and familial identity with Christian belief and practice.

If theologians are wrestling with issues of Christian exclusivism, Christians in the pew are even more confused. In one sense the "ordinary" Christian is far ahead of the theological leadership, for the reality of their everyday lives has drawn many of them willy-nilly into relations with persons of other religions. However, these Christians are often unable to understand theologically their relationships with other religions. They have either not heard of, or cannot accept, the arguments of theologians seeking "a wider ecumenism." Additionally, Paul Knitter has noted that theologians arguing for more inclusive understandings of Christianity are often totally at odds not only with fellow theologians but with Christians in the church. He writes,

> All of these reservations, which come not from the Falwells and Ratzingers, but from some of the more liberal thinkers in our communities, are based on the perceived clash between the new nonabsolute views of Christ and the sensus fidelium. So, if these new christologies [nonabsolute views of Christ] have any future within Christian theology, they need a better ecclesial mediation in order that they might be "received" by the faithful.[16]

Local Christians involved in dialogue are setting aside the theological issues for the sake of practical relationships. It is not that the theological issues are unimportant, but that they are so difficult. Such practical knowledge and experience of other religions may in fact help Christians to envision and articulate a solution to the theological issues and assist with what Knitter calls their "ecclesial mediation."

---

[16] Paul F. Knitter, "Toward a Liberation Theology of Religions," in Hick and Knitter, eds., *The Myth of Christian Uniqueness*, 195 (bracketed material inserted).

Beyond the theological issues surrounding religious exclusivity and Christian understandings of christology, there is another obstacle for American Christians to overcome in accepting religious diversity and coming to know their religious neighbors. This is the long-standing sense of America as a Christian country. While American citizens are strongly committed to the constitutional principle of religious liberty, they also tend to presume that "Christianity" (particularly Protestant Christianity) is "the" religion of our society.[17] That is to say, Christians (particularly Protestants) have a deep sense of Christian entitlement and ideological Christian exclusivism. It can be difficult for some to understand why others make a fuss about posting the Ten Commandments in the public schools, about a Christian prayer before a high school football game, or about including "under God" in the Pledge of Allegiance despite the fact that many citizens have religious beliefs that do not affirm "God." This sense of entitlement and privilege is the product of a long history of Christianity as the dominant or mainstream American culture. A privileged majority is often blind to its privilege; it tends to see its dominant position as a given, simply "the way things are." The problem, of course, is that society is changing, becoming more religiously diverse, and many Christians now know personally members of other religions. These changes can slowly erode unquestioned assumptions.

BEYOND EXCLUSIVISM?

The history of Christian superiority and entitlement (sometimes coupled with racist attitudes, conscious or unconscious) has hampered Christian affirmation of religious diversity and establishment of appropriate relations with non-Christian neighbors. But the changing fabric of American society, the sheer proximity, increasing visibility, and growing dailiness of encounters with people of many faiths are attracting attention. This is no longer an abstract issue confronted only in occasional news stories but a fact of everyday life. As Eck writes,

> It's one thing to be unconcerned about or ignorant of Muslim neighbors on the other side of the world, but when Buddhists are our next-door neighbors, when our children are best friends with Muslim classmates, when a Hindu is running for a seat on the school committee, all of us have a new vested interest in our neighbors, both as citizens and as people of faith.[18]

As we come to have a vested interest in our religious neighbors, our ignorance and lack of understanding become increasingly problematic. Considering that we are now the most religiously diverse society on the planet, the religious illiteracy

---

[17] Catherine L. Albanese discusses how dominant "public Protestantism" has been in United States history (*America: Religions and Religion,* 2nd ed. [Belmont, Calif.: Wadsworth Publishers, 1992], chapter 12).

[18] Eck, *New Religious America,* 6.

of Americans is a significant concern. Without better knowledge of religions we are unprepared to live responsibly as citizens in our society, much less in the world. Nor are we prepared to help Christians in our local parishes who have interfaith marriages, whose daughters and brothers are Buddhists, whose best friend is a Muslim, who practice Hatha Yoga and have no idea how it relates to their Christian practices.

However, few see the need for Christians *as Christians* to understand other religions. Many believe that the primary motivation for establishing a relationship with someone from another religion is to have an opportunity to witness to their Christian faith. However, while it is certainly legitimate for Christians to wish to witness to their faith, they are enjoined by the Ten Commandments not to bear false witness.[19] We need to respect and understand the religions of our neighbors so that we do not unfairly slander or malign them. We need accurate knowledge and solid understanding if we are not to bear false witness; genuine Christian witness cannot be based on false witness against others. The injunction against bearing false witness opens a window for even rather conservative Christians to learn other religions.

My own move beyond a rigid Christian exclusivism is based in my experience. Perhaps because of my personal, everyday experience of diversity in the Bay Area, the very fact of religious diversity seems to compel or demand my understanding and response as a Christian. However, more than the mere fact of diversity, I am moved by my respect and friendship for adherents of other religions whom I have known through my scholarly work. In my thirty-five years as a scholar of East Asian religions, I have been privileged to know remarkable Confucians, Buddhists, and Daoists. These persons are not only splendid representatives of their traditions but also profound and impressive human beings. Because I can sense and appreciate their spirituality and their deep religious wisdom, I simply cannot believe that these people are "outside of salvation."

Theologically, my relationships with these outstanding representatives of their respective traditions have expanded my sense of God's presence. The qualities I experience in these people resonate with what I know of God's love and goodness. As a Christian I believe that God created and is present in the world; I have also come to believe that God can be present in other religions. John Berthrong puts this point very strongly when he writes, "From a monotheistic viewpoint, God created religious pluralism [since God is the Lord of all creation]; our task is to try to understand it theologically, spiritually, and historically."[20]

I understand that neither my experience nor my theological affirmation of God's ability to be present in other religions solves all of the theological problems of Christians relating to other religions. This book is not about resolving those theological issues. It starts from a different premise and is addressed to

---

[19] See John H. Berthrong, *The Divine Deli: Religious Identity in the North American Mosaic* (Maryknoll, N.Y.: Orbis Books, 1999), 45; and Eck, *New Religious America*, 24.

[20] Berthrong, *Divine Deli*, 10-11 (bracketed material inserted to clarify Berthrong's theological stance).

Christians who, like me, feel called to live out our Christian faith in a diverse world by means of respectful relationships with persons of other religions, however much we may still struggle with the theological issues raised by those relationships. My premise is that Christians seeking a more open Christian life can best begin by coming to understand other religions. Understanding (learning other religions) can create a foundation of knowledge from which the difficult and vexing theological issues can in the long run be addressed.

This book argues that learning other religions is a requirement for living as Christians in a religiously diverse world. In doing so, it assumes that such learning both practically and logically comes before the theologian's resolution of theological and ecclesial relations with the other religions. Learning other religions is a way to cultivate appropriate knowledge and relationships without running immediately into the theological walls of Christian exclusivism or treating the dogmas that form us as static ideals. This learning can create a foundation for informed and ongoing theological reflection; in fact, such learning will entail theological reflection, as will be clear in the learning process discussed in chapter 5. To develop the intellectual foundations for the learning process, we now turn to a discussion of learning theories.

2

Thinking about Learning

THE CLASSROOMS FOR WHICH
TEACHERS WERE NOT PREPARED

The last decades of the twentieth century yielded a dramatic change in the classrooms of higher education—colleges, graduate schools, and seminaries. Economic developments, transformations in technology, changes in employment opportunities, and a restructuring of financial aid vastly broadened the population of higher education in this country. In the first half of the twentieth century, students in colleges, graduate schools, and seminaries were overwhelmingly young, white, male, upper middle class, and full-time. The traditional canon of Western literature was taught by means of lectures, essay examinations, and term papers. The educational methods assumed a level of cultural readiness for such learning and prepared students for leadership roles suited to their position in society.

In the second half of the century, expanded financial aid, expectations of employers, increasing necessity for two-career households, and the impact of civil rights and other antidiscriminatory legislation (Title IX, ADA) brought more and more working-class students, women, persons of color, differently abled persons, and immigrants into classrooms. These broadly based students tended to be older, part-time (since many had to hold part-time or full-time jobs before and during their enrollment in school), increasingly nonresidential, and possessed of significant life experience either in this culture or another. Whereas colleges (particularly the more elite colleges) began the century educating primarily young men between the ages of eighteen and twenty-one from relatively privileged social backgrounds to assume positions of influence within society, these same colleges and universities ended the century taking on the general and specialized education of a broad segment of the American work force from diverse social backgrounds and with practical educational goals—a job.

Graduate schools and seminaries also changed rather dramatically. When I entered the Department of East Asian Languages and Cultures at Columbia University in 1967, classes prior to mine had been advised that one had to be a "gentleman of independent means" to pursue the program. My class and subsequent classes entered on fellowships and scholarships from the government and private foundations. We were certainly not "gentlemen of independent means." In my entering class, about two-thirds were women, only 10 percent had parents with graduate educations, a quarter had parents who did not have bachelor's degrees, and 10 percent had one parent who had not graduated from high school. We did not fit the traditional mold, and the faculty had some adjusting to do.

As the diversity of gender, age, cultural, and class backgrounds among students intensified, faculty and administrators in higher education became concerned about the quality of students' work. The language and writing skills of these diverse students did not "match up" to traditional students; faculty saw the new student body as less interested in and less motivated by the traditional curriculum; these students raised questions from their diverse backgrounds and experiences that seemed to some faculty a digression from the agenda of the curriculum. These students did not appear "ready" for the readings, assignments, and approaches to teaching that had worked for the prior fifty years. But of course these were not traditional students.

Brazilian educator Paulo Freire was among the most vocal in claiming that the failures of these students was a failure of their teachers, at least in part a result of "the existing contempt for the learners' cultural identities, the disrespect for popular syntax, and the almost complete disregard for the learners' baggage of experiential knowledge."[1] In other words, the teachers had not yet adjusted to the new social reality in their classrooms; they did not understand their students.

Freire's point was vividly brought home to me in my second year of teaching at Indiana University. Like many faculty, I was both concerned and irritated by intense student anxiety about examinations, complaining that they "didn't know what was expected of them." One day I happened to be listening to public radio and heard an essay on working-class socialization and college expectations. The speaker pointed out that the "standard" college course, centered on mid-term and final examinations, presupposed middle-class socialization. Most middle-class students had been raised to learn and internalize general parental expectations, so that they could understand and meet those expectations with some confidence. Many working-class students, on the other hand, were raised in environments where there were no long-standing, consistent expectations; their parents instead required them to "do what I say, right now". . . "because I say so, that's why." The feedback for such demands was immediate (positive or negative), and tomorrow the parental expectation might be entirely different. Students from such backgrounds had little or no experience with learning, internalizing, and acting with confidence on long-term expectations. They sought immediate and frequent feedback from a teacher (praise or blame) so that they could pick up cues about what would be, in their experience, shifting expectations. As I listened to the radio essay, I realized that it was I who had failed those students, not they who were failing me. I began to structure into my undergraduate courses chances for students gradually to learn, test, and understand my academic expectations so

---

[1] Paulo Freire, *Pedagogy of the Heart* (New York: Continuum, 2000), 62.

that by semester's end they were confident that they understood and could trust those expectations.

The diverse population of students had different needs, different interests, different motivations, and different gifts for learning than the traditional upper-middle-class student population. Unless we were to assert that higher education was possible only for students from a particular social background, educators needed to understand much more deeply how persons of various backgrounds and with various gifts learn.

Educational theorists took up the challenge to consider the implications of the increasingly diverse student population. They recognized that they were facing a new educational world, one that would have to be approached differently. Some theorists reexamined notions of cognitive development and researched diverse ways of learning. Others recognized that that the mere fact of access of previously marginalized students to education did not erase all barriers; they sought to create pedagogies that would empower students and give them voice and agency. Some educators addressed the challenges of diversity for all learners, developing the implications of imagination and narrative as ways to help students enter other worlds and broaden their horizons. Some focused on the challenging process of reacculturating students to develop the language skills needed to negotiate and succeed in broader communities.

DIVERSE WAYS OF LEARNING

One response to the new student populations evolved as scholars reexamined their assumptions about cognitive development and learning patterns. In 1970, William Perry published a highly influential study on cognitive development in the college years, based on interviews with Harvard undergraduates.[2] Perry's book served as a resource for many college teachers seeking to adapt to the new student population. It posited a nine-stage schema of moral and cognitive development for undergraduate learners.

A research team of feminist scholars criticized Perry for assuming in his all-male sample that male models of learning were a universal norm. The team interviewed 135 women from a variety of "educational institutions"—an Ivy League college, an inner-city community college, an "early college" for students who had completed only two years of high school, an alternative high school for students at risk of dropping out, and a number of family agencies for mothers of young children[3]—asking each subject "what was important about life and learning *from her point of view.*"[4] From their analysis of the interviews, the feminist

[2] William G. Perry, *Forms of Intellectual and Ethical Development in the College Years* (New York: Holt, Rinehart, and Winston, 1970).

[3] Mary Field Belenky, Blythe Clinchy, Nancy Goldberger, and Jill Tarule, *Women's Ways of Knowing: The Development of Self, Voice, and Mind* (New York: Basic Books, 1986), 12-13.

[4] Ibid., 11 (italics in original).

team posited seven ways of knowing that reflected the voices and views of their subjects. The seven ways included:

- Silence
- Received Knowledge: Listening to the Voices of Others
- Subjective Knowledge: The Inner Voice
- Subjective Knowledge: The Quest for Self
- Procedural Knowledge: The Voice of Reason
- Procedural Knowledge: Separate and Connected Knowing
- Constructed Knowledge: Integrating the Voices

This study has been both influential and controversial, with controversy swirling around two major issues. First, although the authors claimed they did not intend it, the seven ways of knowing seemed to suggest sequenced stages of development, parallel to those of William Perry. Second, feminist scholars criticized the book for paying insufficient attention to racial and cultural differences among its subjects. Both of these issues were addressed at some length in a subsequent volume, *Knowledge, Difference, and Power: Essays Inspired by Women's Ways of Knowing.*[5] Despite these criticisms and controversies, *Women's Ways of Knowing* remains an important study because of its detailed reporting of the actual views of women from diverse social backgrounds and classes. The many examples cited in the book demonstrate the diverse range of women's social locations and the significant impact of background on learning.

Howard Gardner's research took the issue of diversity beyond differences in class, gender, or cultural background to differences among individual human beings. In 1983 he published *Frames of Mind: A Theory of Multiple Intelligences*, a book that both challenged and stretched traditional understandings of human intelligence.[6]

Gardner initially documented seven intelligences: linguistic, logical-mathematical, spatial, bodily-kinesthetic, musical, interpersonal, and intrapersonal. Gardner studied how all the intelligences manifest themselves in learning, how they function in various careers and professions, and how they are manifested both in "ordinary" learners and in geniuses who have a particular gift in one of the intelligences. In more recent work, Gardner has identified an eighth intelligence (naturalist) and has tentatively considered two additional candidates (spiritual and existential).[7] Gardner maintains that all unimpaired persons use all the intelligences, but each person has a unique combination of relative strengths and weaknesses.

Gardner's research has challenged teachers to be alert for students who

---

[5] Nancy Goldberger, Jill Tarule, Blythe Clinchy, and Mary Belenky, eds., *Knowledge, Difference, and Power: Essays Inspired by Women's Ways of Knowing* (New York.: Basic Books, 1996).

[6] Howard Gardner, *Frames of Mind: A Theory of Multiple Intelligences* (New York: Basic Books, 1983).

[7] Howard Gardner, *Intelligence Reframed: Multiple Intelligences for the 21st Century* (New York: Basic Books, 1999), chapter 4.

strongly favor a specific intelligence and to include materials and learning exercises that engage as many intelligences as possible. By extension, the study also suggested that certain cultural backgrounds or social environments might favor particular intelligences and neglect others; thus Gardner's work became a tool for understanding the learning implications of cultural and environmental differences.

The learning potential of diverse ways of knowing has struck me most dramatically in a doctoral seminar I teach on interdisciplinarity. The seminar engages interdisciplinary theories in order to help students articulate and critically evaluate the interdisciplinarity of their own work. Interdisciplinarity is challenging because it can either be remotely abstract or too close at hand (it's just the way I think!). In presenting various models of interdisciplinary collaboration, one student team brought four sets of Legos, which they mixed up and set out on four tables. They divided the rest of the class into four groups, assigned each a table, and asked each to construct a model of interdisciplinarity and explain their model to the rest of the class. The "teaching" team closely observed the patterns of cooperation that each group developed, reporting back on the group dynamics. The team also noted that none of the groups of interdisciplinary scholars had thought to visit another table to locate the piece that would best complete their model. The student groups worked entirely within their assigned boundaries, like good disciplinary scholars.

This learning experience was extraordinary. Although the medium was unorthodox (how many doctoral students get to work in Legos?), we learned from the challenge of working together within a restricted time frame and restricted to the materials at hand, and we learned immensely from the field analysis by the "teaching team" of each group's dynamics. Each of us left the experience with deeper insight into how to approach and evaluate interdisciplinary work.

LEARNING FOR EMPOWERMENT
OF VOICE AND AGENCY

Paulo Freire did much to revolutionize educational theory with his pedagogical strategies to help poor Brazilian peasants and workers become agents in improving their own lives.[8] Freire published his widely influential *Pedagogy of the Oppressed* in 1970.[9] Freire aspired to "conscienticize" or empower his students through education, to give them agency in shaping their own lives. In order

---

[8] Freire's pedagogy, particularly in its earliest forms, was predicated on Marxist assumptions; hence agency and empowerment were in those early years collective goals for the base community. However, as Freire entered into conversations with and influenced North American educators, the goals of empowerment and agency began to be understood also in individual terms. I am grateful to Kathryn Campbell for her input on this point (personal communication, May 20, 2002).

[9] Paulo Freire, *Pedagogy of the Oppressed* (New York: Herder & Herder, 1970).

to do so, he sought to understand the minds and lives of his students, to engage them actively, and to bring the voices of their experiences into the educational process.

Freire employed an illustration that came to be widely cited by advocates for a new approach to education. He argued that traditional education was founded on a "banking model," seeing the student as an empty vessel into which the teacher deposits knowledge so that the student can call upon it when needed. Lecture, drill, and memorization of information in preparation for tests exemplify the "banking model," which still holds pride of place in many classrooms. The empowerment model, on the other hand, encourages the students to bring their prior experiences (their specific backgrounds and gifts) as assets to the learning process; it builds on those backgrounds and prior experiences to empower the students to understand more critically and act more effectively in work and in life. Learning for empowerment is not about some set curriculum of "information" or "skills," but about critical reflection on experience and the development of effective strategies for creating a better life and a better world. Education is for living, for practice, for active agency in the world.

Freire's critique of the "banking model" recalls John Dewey's criticism of conceptions of knowledge as external to students, a body of facts they store in a warehouse. Instead, Dewey argued that the function of knowledge is to make one particular experience applicable to other life experiences.[10]

bell hooks, an African American womanist and a passionate teacher of English, is an articulate spokesperson for involved and liberative pedagogy, which she calls "education as the practice of freedom." She was inspired by the pedagogy of Paulo Freire, having worked with him and engaged him in dialogue.[11] But while inspired by Freire, her own writings on pedagogy reflect her location as an African American, a feminist, and an educator in North America.

In hooks's first, preintegration all-black school, her black teachers worked with her and other gifted children to nurture their talents and prepare them for work in behalf of the race. Shifting from this environment to integrated white schools, where black students were expected primarily to be quiet and accommodating, was a profound shock. hooks retained her vision of education as enabling despite the fact that integrated public school, college, and graduate school classrooms "began to feel more like prison, a place of punishment and confinement rather than a place of promise and possibility."[12] She had to struggle against increasingly powerful pressures to submit to the authority and hegemony of received views of the white male world.

hooks survived all this with her independent mind and spirit intact and entered the college classroom as a teacher committed to giving her students a taste of education as freedom. Given her own educational odyssey, she was well aware of

---

[10] John Dewey, *Democracy and Education* (New York: Free Press, 1916).

[11] See bell hooks, *Teaching to Transgress: Education as the Practice of Freedom* (New York: Routledge, 1994), chapter 4.

[12] Ibid., 4.

how traditional modes of instruction marginalized, silenced, and "imprisoned" students whose backgrounds and voices were not part of the mainstream. She knew that teaching must change.

> Despite the contemporary focus on multiculturalism in our society, particularly in education, there is not nearly enough practical discussion of ways classroom settings can be transformed so that the learning experience is inclusive. If the effort to respect and honor the social reality and experiences of groups in this society who are nonwhite is to be reflected in a pedagogical process, then as teachers—on all levels, from elementary to university settings—we must acknowledge that our styles of teaching need to change. Let's face it: most of us were taught in classrooms where styles of teaching reflected the notion of a single norm of thought and experience, which we were encouraged to believe was universal. This has been just as true for nonwhite teachers as for white teachers. Most of us learned to teach emulating this model. As a consequence, many teachers are disturbed by the political implications of a multicultural education because they fear losing control in a classroom where there is no one way to approach a subject—only multiple ways and multiple references.[13]

hooks argues that teachers must be prepared for the challenge of transforming their teaching for the sake of their students.

She advocates an "engaged pedagogy," teaching committed to the betterment of students.

> To educate as the practice of freedom is a way of teaching that anyone can learn. That learning process comes easiest to those of us who teach who also believe that there is an aspect of our vocation that is sacred; who believe that our work is not merely to share information, but to share in the intellectual and spiritual growth of our students. To teach in a manner that respects and cares for the souls of our students is essential if we are to provide the necessary conditions where learning can most deeply and intimately begin.[14]

hooks's articulation of engaged pedagogy as a practice of freedom is compatible with the conscienticization of Paulo Freire in that it is an act not merely of transmitting information but also of empowerment, a development of agency. But hooks's definition of empowerment is as much intellectual and spiritual as it is political. Her articulation of the spiritual dimension of teaching has had great influence among theological educators; it lifts the "spiritual" out of the realm of the "private" and "personal" into the context of the learning community.

---

[13] Ibid., 35-36.
[14] Ibid., 13.

Engaged pedagogy requires building a classroom community where learning can flourish. hooks writes,

> Working with a critical pedagogy based on my understanding of Freire's teaching, I enter the classroom with the assumption that we must build a "community" in order to create a climate of openness and intellectual rigor. Rather than focusing on issues of safety, I think that a feeling of community creates a sense that there is a shared commitment and a common good that binds us. What we all ideally share is the desire to learn—to receive actively knowledge that enhances our intellectual development and our capacity to live more fully in the world.[15]

The creation of such a community places the teacher as a learner alongside the students, each engaging the other in order to come to knowledge. The engagement of teacher as learner alongside students undermines the teacher's traditional "authority of expertise." In hooks's model, the authority of the teacher is used to empower students.

The creation of this learning community requires bringing students into active conversation, empowering them to speak, but also teaching them to listen to one another. The teacher must first value the presence of every person and every voice in the classroom. She must also engage the students in the collective effort of learning, speaking, and listening. The teacher must direct students away from sole attention to her voice or from conversing only through the teacher and encourage them to listen and to respond to one another. The engagement and mutual interest require that all bring excitement and passion into the classroom. hooks argues that eros and passion are indispensable to fostering a love of learning. hooks's affirmation of passion stems in part from her feminist denunciation of the mind–body split. Both her teaching and the learning she nurtures are fully embodied; they transform the whole person.

hooks seeks to include all of the voices and perspectives in the classroom. She writes, "knowing from personal experience as a student in predominantly white institutions how easy it is to feel shut out or closed down, I am particularly eager to help create a learning process in the classroom to engage everyone."[16] hooks seeks to bring the multiple voices to contribute to the shared issues at hand, and to enhance the learning experience of the group. When engaged pedagogically, hooks suggests, the telling of experience can help an entire class to better understand the world (facts) and better articulate theory (abstract constructs). In the diverse classroom, different experiences and different ways of knowing contribute to the collective learning effort. hooks's approach to teaching and learning brings critical and intellectual rigor into engagement with multiple embodied experiences.

---

[15] Ibid., 39-40.
[16] Ibid., 86.

An example of hooks's engaged pedagogy seeking to include all voices and to attend to the souls of the students occurred in another seminar on interdisciplinarity. This seminar included a highly educated Kenyan student who was on the verge of preparing his dissertation proposal on the relationships of Christianity, Islam, and Bukusu religions in western Kenya. Patrick faced two challenges in developing his proposal. First, his faculty committee, and indeed his English-speaking audience, were greatly ignorant of Kenyan culture and history; this ignorance made him feel that he had to start from the beginning and explain all of Kenyan culture and history. Second, Patrick's culture conveyed knowledge in the form of vivid oral stories; he thus wanted to tell us "the story of his dissertation." The seminar participants and I first had to listen to Patrick's stories; we had to honor his distinctive voice for developing his ideas. As we listened, we were able to engage him in a conversation that helped him "pour" the substance of his stories (his issues and his passions) into the compact, formal genre of the dissertation proposal. In other words, we helped him to meet the formal requirements of the dissertation proposal without losing his voice or agency, without ceding any of his important and impassioned project.

ENTERING OTHER WORLDS:
LEARNING AND IMAGINATION

The diverse classroom of the late twentieth and early twenty-first centuries challenges not only teachers and the "new" student population but all students of whatever background, for the diversity of the classroom is merely a microcosm of the increasing diversity of the world in which all live and work. Learning in a diverse world requires not merely mastering some set of information but also learning to understand and negotiate areas of human difference, envisioning new ways of being and new possibilities.

Maxine Greene constructs her educational theory on the possibilities of the imagination, building on John Dewey's *Art as Experience*.[17] Although she recognizes that there are many models of teaching and learning, she explains her focus on imagination:

> One of the reasons I have come to concentrate on imagination as a means through which we can assemble a coherent world is that imagination is what, above all, makes empathy possible. It is what enables us to cross the empty spaces between ourselves and those we teachers have called "other" over the years. If those others are willing to give us clues, we can look in some manner through the strangers' eyes and hear through their ears. That is because, of all our cognitive capacities, imagination is the one that per-

---

[17] John Dewey, *Art as Experience* (New York: Minton, Balch, 1934).

mits us to give credence to alternative realities. It allows us to break with the taken for granted, to set aside familiar distinctions and definitions.[18]

Imagination helps us to come to know "the other." She also cites the role of imagination in breaking out of the given, the taken for granted, what Virginia Woolf called the "cotton wool of daily life." Greene comments,

> All depends on breaking free, a leap, and then a question. I would like to claim that this is how learning happens and that the educative task is to create situations in which the young are moved to *begin* to ask, in all the tones of voice there are, "Why?"[19]

Imagination is also an important means by which human beings expand the horizons of their world. Greene writes,

> Most of us can recall the enclave mentality of our early lives and their odd provincialism. We were probably convinced that normal people, "nice people," lived precisely as we did, observed the same rituals, and reacted to events in the same way. It took time before we became acquainted with— and were able to accept—the enormous variety of human lives, the multiplicity of faiths and ways of believing, and the amazing diversity of customs in the world. To come to terms with such additional realities always involves a risk, one many adults are still unwilling to take and to see their children take. If those children do have the imagination to adjust to what they gradually find out about the intersubjective world as they move further and further from the views of their original home, they are bound to reinterpret their early experiences, perhaps to see the course of their lives as carrying out the possible (among numerous possibilities) rather than the necessary.[20]

Imagination, for Greene, is not just the isolated ability to envision bits and pieces of the as-yet unthought, but is rather the faculty that expands our horizons beyond "the givens" and opens up a vast realm of alternatives and possibilities. Imagination has an ethical and social dimension; it opens up the realm of alternative ways of being in the world, creating new possibilities for human community.

Releasing the imaginations of students is aided by encounter with works of imagination in the visual and narrative arts. The visual arts often depict a strug-

---

[18] Maxine Greene, *Releasing the Imagination: Essays on Education, the Arts, and Social Change* (San Francisco: Jossey-Bass, 1995), 3.

[19] Ibid., 5-6, citing Virginia Woolf, *Moments of Being: Unpublished Autobiographical Writings,* ed. J. Schulkind (Orlando, Fla.: Harcourt, 1976), 72 (italics in original).

[20] Ibid., 20 -21.

gle for meaning, as artists respond to challenges in their lives or their artistic worlds. Likewise, narrative arts or texts are opportunities to explore worlds of meaning. Human beings seek to shape their life experiences into narratives (stories) as a way of making meanings; we must "inescapably understand our lives in narrative form, as a 'quest.'"[21]

Narratives, or stories, re-present worlds of meaning; as readers we are able to enter narrative worlds and explore the meanings presented therein. In fact, as readers we help to create the world and meanings in the text. While the author shapes the text by means of his values, interests, and agendas, the reader brings her own experiences, agendas, and interests to the act of reading. The reader's preconceptions are, on the one hand, a lens through which she encounters the text and, on the other hand, are engaged, stretched, or challenged by what she encounters in the text.

Narratives invite us both to enter new realms of experience in the stories told by others, and to construct our own meaning and identity through the elaboration and refinement of our own stories. Storytelling is itself a mode of knowing ourselves and opening ourselves to the stories of others. Feminists and liberation theologians have developed forms of knowing based on personal and collective narratives. Moreover, narrative ethicists have recognized narrative as a key form of moral discourse. Thus the "narrative" knowing Greene celebrates has made its way into several disciplines.[22]

Greene's commitment to narrative, the arts, and imagination presupposes education as understanding, not simply as the assimilation of facts. Learners must enter other worlds and engage other perspectives in conversation.

Many teachers and learners have had extraordinary experiences of the power of imagination in the arts or in narratives to help learners enter other worlds and broaden their horizons. One vivid memory from my own teaching life goes back to an honors course I taught at IU in the early 1980s entitled "Sage and Society in Confucian China." Teaching Confucianism to undergraduates at IU was no mean challenge; these young adults were just asserting their independence of family, and they were by no means ready to engage the Chinese family system or the values of filial piety. After having them read several novels about Chinese families, I asked them to compose a letter from a Confucian father on his death bed, offering his words of wisdom and advice to his family. These young students had never before thought of themselves as parents, or imagined what it would be like to be old, looking back on one's life. The imaginative exercise lifted them out of their present situation and gave them a chance to see life, family, and values from a different generational, religious, and cultural perspective. They all reported that the exercise helped them to see the world from a different point of view.

---

[21] Ibid., 75, citing Charles Taylor, *Sources of the Self: The Making of Modern Identity* (Cambridge, Mass.: Harvard University Press, 1989), 51-52.

[22] I am grateful to James Bretzke, S.J., for raising this point (personal communication, June 6, 2002).

REACCULTURATION: LEARNING AS COLLABORATIVE
CONVERSATION ACROSS LINES OF DIFFERENCE

Kenneth Bruffee has articulated a process by which students from diverse backgrounds can be reacculturated into the broader world of academic discourse. Bruffee relates how as a young assistant professor in 1971 he brashly agreed to become Director of Freshman English during the first year of open admissions at Brooklyn College. He sets the scene:

> In open admissions, some 20,000 new students, many of them lacking the basic skills of reading, writing, and mathematics needed for college work, entered the City University of New York. These new students challenged the university's faculty in ways that often far exceeded the experience, training, and expectations of scholars and scientists bred in the quiet intensity of library carrels and research labs. To most of us it felt like a rout.[23]

In increasing desperation, Bruffee gathered a group of New York area faculty also faced with the challenge of teaching Freshman English in the unprecedented classroom environment of the 1970s. His conversations with these colleagues led him to reconceive fundamentally his model of college learning. Shifting from more traditional models of socialization, "finishing," or "refinement," Bruffee came to understand the classroom as a site of reacculturation.[24] The freshmen, he noted,

> talked, wrote, and behaved in a manner that was perfectly correct and acceptable within the community they were currently members of. . . . Our job as teachers was not in the first instance to "correct" them. . . . Our job as teachers was to find ways to begin and to sustain a much more difficult, painful, and problematical process. . . .[It] was to find out how, in some way and in some measure, to *reacculturate* the students who had been placed in our charge.[25]

That is to say, the professor reacculturates students into the world of academic learning, of the disciplines, of higher education, of critical conversation. The communities the students brought to their college experience were limited, as all

---

[23] Kenneth A. Bruffee, *Collaborative Learning: Higher Education, Interdependence, and the Authority of Knowledge,* 2nd ed. (Baltimore: Johns Hopkins University Press, 1999), 3.

[24] James Bretzke clarifies the correct usage of the term "acculturation" ("Cultural Particularity and the Globalisation of Ethics in Light of Inculturation," *Pacifica* 9 [February 1996]: 79). Enculturation (or sometimes inculturation) refers to the initial insertion of an individual into his or her native culture. Acculturation refers to the cultural change or adaptation that occurs when individuals from two different cultures meet. Bretzke would thus say that Bruffee is discussing acculturation.

[25] Bruffee, *Collaborative Learning,* 5 (italics in original).

communities are. They in turn limited the possibilities and the opportunities of the students:

> Their worlds were closed by walls of words. To be acculturated[26] to those perfectly valid and coherent but entirely local communities alone had severely limited their freedom. It had prepared them for social, political, and economic relations of only the narrowest sort. It had closed them out of relations with other communities, including the broader, highly diverse, integrated American (or for that matter, international) community at large represented in a perhaps minor, but (from their point of view) not insignificant way by a job at the telephone company [which required demonstrated facility in standard English]. One result of this exclusively local acculturation appeared to be that many of our students could not discover their own buried potential and could not achieve the more economically viable and vocationally satisfying lives they aspired to.[27]

So, while teachers need to understand and engage the particular worlds from which their students come, their aim as teachers is to help students enter broader worlds of conversation, understanding, and opportunity, to enable them to discover their potential as learners and to develop the skills needed to achieve their life goals. What a liberal education offers, Bruffee argues, is "having acquired something of the linguistic flexibility needed to negotiate the boundaries of diverse knowledge communities."[28]

Bruffee and his colleagues turned to the writings of Paulo Freire and the feminists, who were using educational strategies to raise consciousness and empower persons to be effective in broader spheres of action. Freire and others helped them to envision a pedagogy of reacculturation. Bruffee writes,

> We learned first that reacculturation is at best extremely difficult to accomplish. . . . What does seem just possible to accomplish is for people to reacculturate themselves by working together. That is, there is a way to sever, weaken, or renegotiate our ties to one or more of the communities we belong to and at the same time gain membership in another community. We can do that if, and it seems in most cases only if, we work collaboratively. What we have to do, it appears, is to organize or join a temporary support or transition group on the way to our goal, as we undergo the trials of changing allegiance from one community to another.[29]

Upon reflection, Bruffee and his colleagues realized this is precisely how they had handled the challenge of fundamentally rethinking the teaching of Freshman English. By extension, this should work for their students.

---

[26] Bretzke would say "enculturated" ("Cultural Particularity and the Globalisation of Ethics," 79).
[27] Bruffee, *Collaborative Learning,* 6-7 (bracketed material inserted).
[28] Ibid., 158.
[29] Ibid., 7-8.

Bruffee proposes that the teacher reconstitute the class into small collaborative learning groups of, optimally, four students each. The teacher assigns the groups collaborative tasks of reading, conversation, and writing. Students would gradually learn to vest authority and trust in this group, and through the group in the class as a whole, and from that class (through the unobtrusive modeling and facilitation of the teacher) in the learning community into which they are being introduced. The small groups (and the larger class) engage in conversations at the boundaries between the communities from which the students came and the community of knowledge into which they are being invited.

The students in the collaborative group come from different learning communities; in fact, each student participates in several communities based on home, church, school, and clubs, to name a few. Bruffee writes,

> This increased awareness of community boundaries is key to students' development in collaborative learning. . . . They find, invent, or borrow transitional terms with which to mediate differences at the boundaries among the several nested groups they are members of. As they do so— indeed, in order to do so—they tend to soften these differences and penetrate those boundaries. . . . By helping one another feel more comfortable in crossing these boundaries, they initiate one another into the larger discourse communities they are joining. But they do not so much abandon the knowledge communities they were raised in as learn how to negotiate new relationships with those familiar old communities they were raised in, while at the same time negotiating their way into new communities a college education invites them to join.[30]

The task of the collaborative group is translation: first, the creation of transitional or border languages to assist the students in moving from their prior languages of knowledge to the language of the "larger" learning community, and then practicing and gaining facility in the language and mores of this new community until each learner has internalized it for his own use. For the collaboration of these transitional communities to be educationally effective, Bruffee notes, students must learn to vest confidence and authority not solely or even primarily in the teacher, but in their peers and ultimately in themselves. They have to develop confidence in the collaborative process, in the power of conversation.

Bruffee affirms and builds on Richard Rorty's understanding of knowledge as socially justified belief. Rorty argued for a shift from knowledge in relation to objects (epistemology) to knowledge in relationship to understanding confirmed in conversation or argument with peers (hermeneutics). Knowledge, for Rorty, was primarily a matter of conversation and social practice.[31] He wrote,

> If . . . we think of "rational certainty" as a matter of victory in argument rather than of relation to an object known, we shall look toward our inter-

---

[30] Ibid., 47.
[31] Richard Rorty, *Philosophy and the Mirror of Nature* (Princeton: Princeton University Press, 1979), 171.

locutors rather than to our faculties for the explanation of the phenomenon. If we think of our certainty about the Pythagorean Theorem as our confidence, based on experience with arguments on such matters, that nobody will find an objection to the premises from which we infer it, then we shall not seek to explain it by relation of reason to triangularity. Our certainty will be a matter of conversation between persons.[32]

The language of a knowledge community constitutes the techniques and discursive practices by which it justifies its beliefs. Thus, learning the language of the broader knowledge community gives learners access to the justification of its beliefs.[33]

The radical implication of Rorty's position, which Bruffee endorses, is that knowledge is socially constructed, not something already in the world to be discovered; it is nonfoundational. Rorty distinguishes collaborative learning tasks from "foundational" learning tasks, tasks such as jigsaw puzzles, with a predetermined right answer reached by following a predetermined method. Tasks appropriate to collaborative learning are, by contrast, "nonfoundational, constructive, tool-making tasks." There is no single right answer, but a variety of responses that will be constructed by the collaborative work of the students.[34] The shift to nonfoundational, socially constructed knowledge requires us all to learn a new language, new habits of thinking.

Teaching for reacculturation, then, requires that the teacher trust the collaborative learning process. Although teachers are trained in and represent the learning community of their disciplines, their authority as teachers lies more in their role as translators who can help mediate between the several languages of knowledge communities brought by the students and the language of the community of knowledge the students are invited to enter. The authority of professors as scholars in their disciplines lies in their mastery of the discipline's central discourse, but their authority as teachers lies in their skill at the boundaries between their disciplines and the many worlds from which their students come. Bruffee writes,

> Mere chemists have to be able to talk comprehensibly as chemists with other chemists and, on occasion, perhaps, to a physicist, astronomer, biologist, or lawyer. *Teachers* of college and university chemistry also have to be able to talk comprehensibly as chemists with all the Trekkies, romance novel readers, canoers, computer hackers, fast-food restaurant assistant managers, and football players who aspire to become chemists or at least learn something about chemistry.[35]

Bruffee, then, urges teachers to be translators and facilitators, willing to work at the boundaries between learning communities and to help the students to collab-

---

[32] Ibid., 156-57.

[33] Bruffee, *Collaborative Learning,* 236.

[34] Ibid., 30, referring to Richard Rorty, *Contingency, Irony, and Solidarity* (Cambridge: Cambridge University Press, 1989), 11-12.

[35] Ibid., 71 (italics in original).

orate to create transitional languages in order to enter the larger learning community. He urges them to design collaborative learning tasks and then to interfere as little as possible with the small groups, letting the social construction of knowledge follow its course.

His approach to teaching entails the encouragement and facilitation of conversation, first actual and then internalized within the students, which will result in their learning a new way of thinking and speaking—not merely the "jargon" and "vocabulary" of a discipline but the fluency of its language and its forms of justification of belief.

Bruffee's articulation of the process of collaborative learning is extraordinarily helpful in the classroom. Long before I read his book, I was searching for ways to help timid or passive undergraduates engage Chinese texts and religious ideas in classes of forty to fifty students. I learned to assign students to write a brief interpretation of a passage informally in preparation for class, and then have them discuss their papers in groups of three or four for at least thirty minutes before turning to plenary discussion. The written assignment assured that shy students had articulated their ideas, committing them to paper before appearing in class. The small group discussions taught students that there were a range of interpretations and that they could learn from one another, honing their ideas and sharpening their language through conversation. This conversation among the students enabled them to develop language by means of which they could interpret the texts. These collaborative exercises not only sharpened each student's understanding of the text, but it helped them voice their ideas or their questions. It helped them transcend their paralysis before a text that seemed to them too strange to be understood.

CONCLUSION

The educational theorists in this chapter all responded to the implications of the increasingly diverse classrooms of the late twentieth century. Although they focused on different issues, their work collectively highlights six critical aspects of learning in a diverse world: (1) building on the diversity of learners' experiences; (2) empowering learners by developing voice and agency; (3) entering other worlds through art and narrative so that learners broaden their horizons and cross boundaries; (4) engaging understanding and interpretation, not merely the mastery of information; (5) developing linguistic flexibility through conversation—speaking, listening, and constructing new knowledge; (6) establishing community and relationships to act effectively in the world.

As noted in the preface, these educational theories do not represent the full spectrum of educational ideas. They are, however, approaches that can be particularly helpful in articulating the process of Christians learning another religion. We next turn to the field of comparative religions, in which the issues involved in understanding religious difference have been debated and addressed.

3

Learning Religions

The field of the study of religions, usually called comparative religions or religious studies, takes as its subject matter the diverse religious traditions of humankind. Although cultural exchange has drawn human beings into contact with other religions for millennia, the formal study of other religions is relatively recent. In Europe Max Müller announced the imminent creation of a new field, or more precisely a new "science," in a lecture in 1870:

> A Science of Religion, based on an impartial and truly scientific comparison of all, or at all events, of the most important, religions of mankind, is now only a question of time. . . . It becomes therefore the duty of those who have devoted their life to the study of the principal religions of the world in their original documents, and who value religion and reverence it in whatever form it may present itself, to take possession of this new territory in the name of true science.[1]

Although the nascent field was shaped by the values, assumptions, biases, and agendas of its Victorian, liberal Christian founders, it brought into academic and public discourse the issues of religious otherness. As the field has evolved over the last 130-odd years, scholars have continued to develop methods for understanding religious difference.

This chapter addresses four themes in the study of religions that are of particular relevance to this book: (1) religious context and particularity; (2) the importance of difference; (3) the intersubjective as the aspect of religions accessible to study; and (4) power and human relationships in the study of religions. Throughout the chapter I will move rather seamlessly from the scholar's study of religions to the student's learning of religions. Granted, scholars must be concerned with research methods and hold themselves to rigorous standards of linguistic, textual, and cultural competence, but they are still learning religions. The principles for

---

[1] Max Müller, *Introduction to the Science of Religion: Four Lectures Delivered at the Royal Institute* (London: Longmans, Green, 1873), 34ff., cited in Eric J. Sharpe, *Comparative Religion: A History*, 2nd ed. (Chicago: Open Court Publishing, 1986), xi. The 1870 lecture was published in 1873.

scholars and learners are fundamentally the same, at least on the nontechnical level discussed in this chapter. The last section of the chapter will draw out general principles for learning other religions and relate them to the principles of teaching and learning discussed in the previous chapter.

BEYOND "SCIENCE": RELIGIOUS CONTEXT AND PARTICULARITY

In the decade leading up to Max Müller's lecture, the study of religions was fundamentally changed when the concept of evolution burst onto the European intellectual scene. Science and evolution challenged the Christian churches' acceptance of divine revelation in its literal biblical form. Science and evolution were seen as threats to the foundation of Christian faith and civilization because they challenged biblical views of creation and human history.

European intellectuals sought to reconcile the ideas of science and evolution with views of the superiority of European civilization and religion. Darwin's evolutionary theories were rather crudely applied by sociologists and anthropologists to place human societies along an evolutionary scale from primitive, childlike societies to civilized, mature societies such as those in Europe. Early theorists of totemism and magic sought the "origins" of religion in "primitive" or "childlike" forms that eventually matured or flourished into theistic and finally monotheistic religions. The religious beliefs and practices of various cultures were painted with a very broad brush, placing them along the scholars' evolutionary scale. Some theorists assumed that the "form" or "stage" of religion reflected the stage of cultural development.

In liberal Christian circles of the nineteenth and early twentieth centuries, Christian views were largely reconciled to evolutionary thinking by a shift in the understanding of revelation. Instead of viewing revelation as fixed in the Bible, God was understood as revealing God's self in history, not only in biblical times but continuously. Such a view allowed for an evolution of Christian thinking and for the accommodation of historical and cultural change. It also allowed for a more sympathetic view of other religions.

The early shapers of the study of religions all hailed from this liberal Christian camp. While they shared a commitment to the rigorous study of religion based on extensive knowledge of religious texts, they also saw themselves as theologians first and foremost. They shared the belief of Nathan Soderblom that "every scientific study of religion, provided that it is carried out with competence and directed toward a worthy object, must—with or against the will of the scholar, consciously or unconsciously—serve the cause of religion."[2] These liberal Christians saw no ultimate conflict between the thoroughgoing and sympa-

---

[2] Nathan Soderblom, *Studiet av religionen* (Stockholm: P. A. Norstedt & Soners, 1916), 24, cited in Sharpe, *Comparative Religion,* 156.

thetic study of other religions and their own Christian faith, for they believed that the scientific application of reason would ultimately vindicate Christianity.[3]

Thus, the early practice of the "science" of religion posited broad evolutionary principles undergirded by assumptions of the superiority of Western civilization and Christianity. The "scientific" scholar broadly analyzed particular religions, using categories based on Western and Christian culture, as instances of the development of religion (singular) in human civilization. In other words, they constructed a "story of religion" that reinforced their Christian and cultural assumptions. They abstracted religions into essences or objects of study to gain so-called objective knowledge through "scientific methods."[4] This view of "science" has been exposed and critiqued in contemporary philosophy of science.

In the past fifty years, scholars of religions have turned away from the search for grand patterns in the development of religion, recognizing both that they mask hidden agendas of cultural and religious superiority and that they fail to do justice to particular religions in their historical and cultural contexts. In part this was the result of a growing knowledge of particular religions; increasing numbers of scholars, both Western and non-Western, studied the texts, histories, and practices of various religious traditions and historical contexts. Increasing knowledge of religious and cultural particularities undermined the credibility of broad patterns across religions.

Some scholars specialized in area studies, studying one particular religious context, learning its language, culture, and history in depth, with no attention to the broader history of religions or the general issues of understanding religious difference. Others, however, sought to ground the comparative study of religions in historical contexts, insisting that its purpose was not the generation of general laws or patterns of religion but rather the interpretation of human meaning.

Jonathan Z. Smith is one of the most influential voices for the comparative study of religions. On the one hand, he is a trenchant critic of almost all current practices of comparison, charging that they are more "magical" than scholarly:

[A]s practiced by scholarship, *comparison has been chiefly the affair of the recollection of similarity. The chief explanation for the significance of comparison has been contiguity.* The procedure is homeopathic. The theory is built on contagion. The issue of difference has been all but forgotten.[5]

Such comparisons are really loose patterns of association emanating from the mind of the scholar.

On the other hand, Smith identifies two principles necessary for sound com-

---

[3] My discussion of the history of the field of comparative religions to this point is deeply indebted to Sharpe's account in *Comparative Religion.*

[4] Gavin Flood, *Beyond Phenomenology: Rethinking the Study of Religion* (London: Cassell, 1999), 9.

[5] Jonathan Z. Smith, *Imagining Religion: From Babylon to Jonestown* (Chicago: University of Chicago Press, 1982), 21 (italics in original).

parisons. Comparisons must attend first to the historical location and particularity of religions, adequately describing how the various elements of a religion find meaning in their particular context. Second, students of religion need a sophisticated and complex view of the systems or complexes that form a religion. Comparisons that lift a single element out of the historical and systematic context may compare something, but it is not religion. Religion is embedded in the many systems and complexes of a cultural context. Comparative studies of religion have tended to honor one of these principles, Smith claims, but seldom both at the same time. "We have yet to develop a responsible alternative: the integration of a complex notion of pattern and system with an equally complex notion of history."[6]

Jonathan Z. Smith's position seems to suggest that valid comparisons would have to put contextualized, grounded religious meanings (and the beliefs and practices on which they are based) into a mutually critical "conversation." By extension, to understand another religion is to attend to its otherness, to learn what it means to persons in that particular context, and how that meaning is shaped by the context. Wilfred Cantwell Smith makes a related point when he argues that scholarship of religion has turned from merely uncovering material or data to plumbing its human significance:

> Not the tribal dance, so much as what happens to the African dancing; not the caste system, so much as what kind of person the Hindu becomes within it, or without it; not the events at Sinai, so much as what role the recounting of those events has played in Jewish life over various centuries since.[7]

Both Smiths, Jonathan Z. and Wilfred Cantwell, understand religion as grounded in the particular historical contexts. Jonathan Z. tends to stress the large picture, the "systems and complexes" that form religion in a particular context, while Wilfred Cantwell tends to stress the role of religion in human lives. The latter writes, "The faith of Buddhists does not lie in the data of the Buddhist tradition; it lies . . . in what tradition means to people; in what the universe means to them, in light of that tradition."[8] Together the two Smiths represent well the move among scholars of religion to stress that religion is always grounded in and shaped by a particular context.

Historically grounded religions naturally change and evolve as contexts change; they are not fixed or static. Moreover, they are internally diverse, as there are multiple "contexts" or perspectives within any religion. This is dramatically true of "world" religions, such as Islam, Buddhism, or Christianity, which have adapted to and been influenced by a variety of cultural and historical contexts.

---

[6] Ibid., 29.

[7] Wilfred Cantwell Smith, *Towards a World Theology: Faith and the Comparative History of Religion* (Philadelphia: Westminster Press, 1981; Maryknoll, N.Y.: Orbis Books, 1989), 48.

[8] Ibid., 47.

But all religions, however geographically limited, are internally diverse because their members are older and younger, male and female, rich and poor, powerful and ordinary, pious or casual about religion. One cannot understand Buddhism, Christianity, Islam, or Shinto as a whole; each of these contains diverse voices, perspectives, practices, and experiences.

Wilfred Cantwell Smith helpfully distinguishes between the vast "cumulative tradition" of, say, Buddhism and the fragment of it represented by any particular person, text, or group we might study:

> We have here an historical involvement, a complex: formed by a continu-ing interaction of personal faith, on the one hand, and, on the other, of cer-tain things which I call dynamically a "cumulative tradition," meaning by "tradition" quite literally that array of observables that is handed on. . . . That segment of the cumulative tradition that is available and germane to any particular Buddhist person or group constitutes the Buddhist context of their life.[9]

This point is important at several levels and provides an apt way of summarizing the implications of historical particularity in the study of religions.

First, the cumulative tradition of a religion is too vast and internally diverse (historically, culturally, socially) to be neatly summarized. It contains many voices, perspectives, moments, and disagreements in the historical development of a tradition. Thus, succinct summaries of any religion are misleading and mask the richness and diversity of the religion. Second, any particular group, person, or text represents only a particular piece of the vast cumulative tradition; it does not speak for the religion as a whole. On the other hand, the very location of the group, person, or text, once acknowledged and understood, shapes the meanings of religious life and belief in that context. In other words, the locatedness of a religious voice provides a genuine perspective on the religion, but it is never the only perspective on the religion. Third, because of the particularity and located-ness of voices, understanding another religion will require engagement with the multiple voices and perspectives of the religion. We can never engage with all of the voices, but engagement with multiple voices provides a fuller and more nuanced understanding of a religion in its internal diversity.

BEYOND EMPATHY:
THE IMPORTANCE OF DIFFERENCE

Early scholars of the new field worried about how to extend adequate sympa-thy in their study of other religions. John Nicol Farquhar wrote,

> An unsympathetic student of the Gospels inevitably misinterprets them; and the same is true of an unsympathetic student of the Upanishads, the

---

[9] Ibid., 24-25.

Mahabharata, or the Puranas. The attitude of the great scholars of the West to Hindu literature ought to be the ideal of every Missionary. I do not mean that he will necessarily praise what they praise and condemn what they condemn: let him adopt their attitude of mind, their patience, their eagerness to understand even that which is furthest away from their own conceptions, and the penetrating sympathy which enables them to look at an ancient text with the eyes of those who first read it.[10]

Farquhar aspires to the ideal of empathy: adopting the attitude of mind, patience, and eagerness of the other to "look at an ancient text with the eyes of those who first read it." He sought, as some might say today, to "walk a thousand miles in their moccasins."

However well intentioned, the ideal of empathy is problematic, for it severely underestimates the challenge of understanding across lines of difference. Empathy, looking with the eyes of another, is impossible. The point is articulated well by anthropologist Clifford Geertz. The ethnographer (or scholar of religions) "does not, and in my opinion, largely cannot, perceive what his informants perceive. What he perceives, and that uncertainly enough, is what they perceive 'with'—or 'by means of,' or 'through' . . . or whatever the word should be."[11] He reports on his own experience. "In each case, I have tried to get at [cross-cultural understanding] not by imagining myself someone else, a rice peasant or a tribal sheikh, and then seeing what I thought, but by searching out and analyzing the symbolic forms—words, images, institutions, behaviors—in terms of which, in each place, people actually represented themselves to themselves and to one another."[12]

In place of sympathy or empathy, seeing *myself* as the other—and thus still looking through my own cultural and experiential lenses—it is important to attend to the particular words, images, and behaviors through which the other represents himself. How is meaning expressed, lived out, understood, and articulated in the context I am seeking to understand? Attending to the particular words, images, and behaviors important in the other context helps me to acknowledge the particularity, the difference, of the religion I am trying to understand.

In the last chapter, we quoted Maxine Greene's statement that imagination makes empathy possible.

It is what enables us to cross the empty spaces between ourselves and those we teachers have called "other" over the years. If those others are willing to give us clues, we can look in some manner through the strangers' eyes and hear through their ears. That is because, of all our cognitive capacities,

---

[10] Eric J. Sharpe, *J. N. Farquhar, A Memoir* (Calcutta, 1962), 127ff. (cited in Sharpe, *Comparative Religion,* 153).

[11] Clifford Geertz, *Local Knowledge: Further Essays in Interpretive Anthropology,* 2nd ed. (New York: Basic Books, 2000), 58.

[12] Ibid., 58.

imagination is the one that permits us to give credence to alternate realities. It allows us to break with the taken for granted, to set aside familiar distinctions and definitions.[13]

Greene's concept of empathy is carefully nuanced. If one attends only to the first two sentences of this quotation, she seems to be advocating the "empathy" or "sympathy" expressed by Farquhar. However, Greene qualifies her position in two important ways: learners have to receive clues from others, and their imaginative grasp will always be partial. It is important to attend to the clues (the particular language, behaviors, symbols) that the other provides so as to attempt to understand the distinctive difference of the other. Further, it is important to recognize that we can only understand "in some manner," to a certain degree.

Jonathan Z. Smith, as we saw, criticized many scholars of religions for focusing solely on similarities, lifting out of context threads or themes that seemed familiar to them in some other religion and forgetting the differences. Clifford Geertz would agree with Smith on that point, and he has significantly influenced scholars of religion in his call for "thick description" of religious beliefs and practices as they are embedded in their social contexts. But description in itself is not enough. One can understand the other religion only by engaging the distinctive language, practices, and behaviors to see how people make meaning of them in their particular context. This is, Geertz notes, a matter of interpretation or hermeneutics. He writes,

> I am not engaged in a deductive enterprise in which a whole structure of thought and practice is seen to flow, according to some implicit logic or other, from a few general ideas, sometimes called postulates, but in an hermeneutic one—one in which such ideas are used as a more or less handy way into understanding the social institutions and cultural formulations that surround them and give them meaning.[14]

As the scholar attends to the distinctive language, patterns, and behavior in the context, she gradually sees or hears how these characteristics are given meaning in that context. The distinctive language or behaviors become the "handles" around which understanding begins to emerge. The difference or foreignness of the language or behavior underscores the challenge of understanding, the gap between the learner's prior experience and this religious other. Attending to the differences, the gap, illustrates what needs to be learned; it challenges the learner to grapple with new words, behaviors, and meanings until some degree of understanding begins to emerge. A learner's tentative and initial understanding of a religion must be subject to correction by the specific texts, terms, and distinctive perspectives of the religion. That requires attention to and respect for difference.

---

[13] Maxine Greene, *Releasing the Imagination: Essays on Education, the Arts, and Social Change* (San Francisco: Jossey-Bass, 1995), 3.

[14] Geertz, *Local Knowledge,* 186-87.

BEYOND THE RELIGIOUS MIND:
WHAT ASPECTS OF RELIGION CAN BE STUDIED?

Some scholars of religion have focused their attention on subjective states of the religious person. As one scholar wrote, "Let us never forget that there exists no other reality than the faith of the believer."[15] Two influential scholars sought to articulate the distinctive feelings or consciousness of the religious person. Rudolf Otto argued that religious experience lay in the awe experienced in the face of the numinous, the *mysterium tremendum*, which was wholly other. His book *The Idea of the Holy* attained nearly canonical status for early-twentieth-century students of religion.[16] Mircea Eliade was also enormously influential for his vast scholarship on the religious person, or *homo religiosus*, who experiences hierophanies, irruptions of the sacred into the world of the profane.[17] Although Eliade has been criticized on a number of grounds, his vast corpus has a wide readership among students of religion intent upon understanding "the religious mind." In part this reflects the interest among students of religion in religious experience, a set of feelings, or a particular form of consciousness.

The problem with such approaches is that learners do not have access to feelings or forms of consciousness of others. They cannot directly engage their faith, their experience, their awe, their hierophanies. They can only engage what people say or write about such experiences or witness their behavior during such experiences. Thus, Gavin Flood argues that religion can be studied only by means of "intersubjective performance in which consciousness is not central."[18] By intersubjective performance, Flood means such items as ritual structure and performed narratives, those aspects of religious life that are central to its cultural expression and are communicated among persons. While some argue that such cultural expressions are the only appropriate data of the human and social sciences, Flood argues for a dialogical and interpretive approach to the study of religious meaning. He cites Mikhail Bakhtin in arguing that our only access to the consciousness of others is dialogical. Bakhtin wrote, "The consciousness of other people cannot be perceived, analyzed, defined as objects or as things—one can only relate to them dialogically. To think about them means to talk with them."[19] Flood sees research and study as a conversation with texts and persons.

---

[15] William Brede Kristensen, *Religionshistorik studium* (Oslo, 1954), 27, cited in Sharpe, *Comparative Religion*, 228.

[16] Rudolph Otto, *The Idea of the Holy: An Inquiry into the Non-rational Factor in the Idea of the Divine and Its Relation to the Rational,* trans. John W. Harvey (London: Oxford University Press, 1950). Originally published 1923.

[17] Although his corpus is vast, the idea of *homo religiosus* was famously introduced in his classic *The Sacred and the Profane: The Nature of Religion*, trans. Willard R. Trask (New York: Harcourt, Brace, and World, 1959).

[18] Flood, *Beyond Phenomenology*, 107-8.

[19] Mikhail Bakhtin, *Problems of Dostoyevsky's Poetics* (Minneapolis: University of Minnesota Press, 1984), 68, cited in Flood, *Beyond Phenomenology,* 111.

The criticism of the study of religious consciousness serves to remind students of religion about the limits of their sources for the understanding of religions. We have access only to cultural expressions of religion: statements, writings, practices, artifacts, and symbols. We do not have access to internal states of mind, nor to the sacred or other ultimate realities that these religions claim. We learn what religious persons believe, say, and do, and how they express the significance of religion in their lives.

BEYOND THE POSTS:[20] POWER AND HUMAN RELATIONSHIPS IN THE STUDY OF RELIGIONS

The movement of peoples across the globe and the changing demography of higher education in the United States had a significant impact on the study of religions. On a very practical level, faculty who taught world's religions suddenly found that representatives of those religions were present in the classroom; they were not simply teaching Christians and Jews about religions elsewhere in the world. The learning community of the classroom was itself religiously diverse. Over time, the broader representation in higher education in the United States and abroad produced new directions in scholarship—scholarship representing voices and points of view previously underrepresented in the academy. This more representative scholarship raised new issues for the study of religions, challenging traditional assumptions and practices.

One set of challenges came from a group of scholars often identified as postcolonialists. As former colonies achieved independence, they produced their own scholars, who were sharply critical of Euroamerican scholarship examining their cultures. They criticized anthropologists, who, like scholars of religions, study the values, beliefs, and practices of many cultures. The analytical eye of anthropology, they noted, was not turned upon mainstream European and North American cultures; anthropology studied only "the other," those considered inferior to "us." Moreover, anthropologists in the field treated those they studied as "objects" rather than as collaborators, extracting information and then producing explanations "nonsensical" in the eyes of their informants. Although anthropologists entered communities and lived in them temporarily to conduct fieldwork, their scholarship did not treat the people with whom they lived and worked as partners, and their work did not reflect the voices of their informants.[21]

The same charges were easily extended to the study of religions.[22] Studies of

---

[20] I borrow this phrase from the title of Barbara A. Holdrege's essay "What's Beyond the Post? Comparative Analysis as Critical Method," in *A Magic Still Dwells: Comparative Religion in the Postmodern Age*, ed. Kimberley C. Patton and Benjamin C. Ray (Berkeley: University of California Press, 2000), 77-91.

[21] Talal Asad, *Anthropology and the Colonial Encounter* (New York: Humanities Press, 1973).

[22] Talal Asad turned his critical eye on the study of religions in *Genealogies of Religion: Discipline and Reasons of Power in Christianity and Islam* (Baltimore: Johns Hopkins University Press, 1993).

Christianity were conducted under the rubrics of history and theology, sometimes of sociology, but "comparative religion" tended to be reserved for "other" religions. And yet, many noted, the categories used by comparativists almost all reflected Christian (and, even more, Protestant) understandings of "religion." Many comparativists still limited their study to religious texts, and their interpretations of those texts, while philologically rigorous, were often cast in the interpretive categories of "Western" understandings of religion. Had comparative religionists been engaged in constructing "others" as less mature versions of themselves?

Edward Said's *Orientalism* raised serious issues about the study of Near Eastern and Asian religions by Europeans and North Americans. In this volume, he traces and analyzes a British and French (and later American) tradition of scholars studying "the Orient" and its traditions. Said argues that the development of scholarship on religions was closely tied to the imperial designs and intentions of European powers and later the United States. Indeed, Said argues that all scholarship is embedded in time and culture and that scholars need to be more attentive to the ways in which their scholarship is shaped by and contributes to the social, political, and economic context in which it is produced.

Said lists four main characteristics of orientalism: (1) positing an absolute and systematic difference between West (superior) and East (inferior); (2) favoring abstractions about the Orient based on classical texts rather than evidence drawn from the contemporary Orient; (3) assuming that the Orient is eternal, uniform, and incapable of defining itself, thus requiring Western scholarship to interpret and re-present it; (4) working on the assumption that the Orient is either something to be feared (the Yellow Peril) or controlled (by occupation or research).[23]

Postcolonialism and orientalism seek to disclose the hidden power assumptions in research on and study of others by those in the West. These scholars suggest that knowledge has been used as a form of mastery, either to control subjugated peoples (as in the colonial era) or to define "us" as culturally superior to them, thus shoring up our sense of privilege. It is also a form of mastery because the Western orientalist scholar presumes to speak for the other, who remains voiceless and disenfranchised, and the Western student believes that the Western scholar's interpretation gives one a coherent grasp of (hold on) the other. The colonialist and orientalist scholars rely on ancient texts in their libraries believed to capture the early (and thus "true") teachings of the religion; they do not offer their armchair reconstructions for correction by the living adherents of the religions. While some of the postcolonial and orientalist charges can be exaggerated or overblown, they nonetheless highlight serious issues that the field has sought to address.

A second challenge comes from a vast literature collectively termed "postmodernism." The meaning and even appropriateness of the term are the subject of heated and ongoing debates, and I do not wish to wade into that minefield.

---

[23] Edward W. Said, *Orientalism* (New York: Vintage Books, 1979), 300-301.

Here I need only lift up a few of the issues that have significant implications (and challenges) for the study of religions.

Postmodernism is suspicious of grand narratives and universals (essences, patterns, metaphysical foundations), favoring instead particularity and difference. Postmodernists see in the postulation of universals a claim to power and domination, an attempt to ignore, erase, or efface the difference of exceptions or nondominant voices. This suspicion of universals and grand narratives mitigates against the postulation of universal patterns or general laws in comparative religion and tends to support those who argue for the differences among religions, emphasizing their irreducible distinctiveness. Taken to its extreme, postmodernism would deny the possibility of understanding other religions.

The celebration of difference and the particular also challenges any notion of a unitary religious tradition. Postmodernists would stress the tensions, debates, and differences within "a tradition" both across history and at any given moment. Thus "Buddhism," "Hinduism," and "Islam" are disclosed as essentializations of what are, in fact, contended and diverse traditions with a plethora of views and practices. Feminist studies and social history have also challenged conventional definitions of tradition. Are we to rely on authoritative texts and views of religious authorities, or will we better understand religion through popular devotional practices, folktales and popular literature, the arts, or local variations of beliefs and practices?

Postmodernism requires a critical reading of texts—both actual texts and "cultural" texts such as practices—looking for the fissures, the gaps, what is not said, and always asking questions about power and voice. By whom was the text produced and for what purpose? What was left out? Who was silenced in order to produce the text? And what interests do the omitted or silenced materials represent? Students of religion are challenged not to take religions at face value but to observe shrewdly how different interests are represented or suppressed at every turn.

Postcolonialism, taken to an extreme, can intimidate Western scholars or students from engaging other religions. Postmodernism, taken to an extreme, can make such studies difficult, if not impossible. The picture can be bleakly painted:

> The substantial and often well-founded charges brought against the comparative method are many: intellectual imperialism, universalism, theological foundationalism, and anti-contextualism. In particular, the work of Mircea Eliade, the late doyen of history of religions, is held to be unredeemable, based as it is on a vision of a universal, transcendent "sacred" refracted in the ritual and mythic behavior of a cross-cultural archetype called *Homo religiosus.*[24]

However, scholars of religion, while acknowledging the merit of some of the charges against past practices, have sought to redefine their principles and prac-

---

[24] Kimberley C. Patton and Benjamin C. Ray, "Introduction," in *A Magic Still Dwells,* ed. Patton and Ray, 1-2.

tices so as to navigate a channel between the errors of nineteenth-century "scientific" study, on the one hand, and the errors exposed by postcolonialism and postmodernism, on the other.

The new approaches include the principles we have already discussed: attention to historical particularity and to difference, and adopting a dialogical and interpretive approach through engaging conversationally with the voices or situated narratives of religions. However, "beyond the post" scholars also attend to issues of power. First, the situatedness of the scholar or learner, on the one hand, and of the voices of religion on the other. What forces shape or constrain the assumptions, views, and actions of both parties? What motivations allow them to engage in mutual conversation? Second, scholars of religion do not presume to speak for the religions they study. They listen to many voices of adherents and have their views corrected. They propose no grand narratives, universal laws, or hard and fast conclusions. Their knowledge is always provisional, nonfinal, merely an interpretation.[25] Third, they respect difference as a way of respecting the voices and perspectives of others. Those perspectives are not reducible to any broad unity that would erase distinctive perspectives. Fourth, they seek to work collaboratively and dialogically with representatives of other religions. "For scholars of religion this means taking seriously the fact that there are people on both sides, all sides, of the process of understanding."[26] Finally, they recognize an ethical dimension in the study of religions, both in the breaking down of stereotypes of the "other" and in engaging the moral issues that face other communities, not speaking for them but standing with them.[27]

The purpose of the "beyond the post" study of religions is "not to reach closure in service of a particular theory, nor to achieve moral judgment or to gain intellectual control over the 'other,' but to empower mutual dialogue and the quest for understanding . . . not to create more generic patterns of the sacred in support of grand theories but to enlarge our understanding of religion in all of its variety and, in the process, to gain renewed insight into ourselves and others."[28]

PRACTICAL IMPLICATIONS
FOR LEARNING RELIGIONS

The discussion in this chapter may have seemed theoretical to some readers, but the issues discussed have significant ramifications for teaching and learning religions.

The importance of religious context and particularity seriously challenges the succinct summaries of religions often provided by introductory texts for world

---

[25] Ibid., 4.

[26] Diana L. Eck, "Dialogue and Method: Reconstructing the Study of Religion," in *A Magic Still Dwells,* ed. Patton and Ray, 140.

[27] Patton and Ray, "Introduction," 17.

[28] Ibid., 17-18.

religions courses. Religions have too often been presented as a few key teachings or practices, or one moment or instance in the religion's history. Often the period of the "founder" has been presented as though it defined the entire religion. Teachers and learners are challenged to engage multiple voices and contexts. On a very different level, teachers today often find in their classrooms representatives of the religions they are teaching. For example, Buddhist students may have learned their Buddhism from family practices and a few festivals, rather than from the canonical texts and philosophical ideas the teacher has studied. Thus the teacher and the class are directly confronted with two very different fragmentary perspectives on the cumulative tradition of Buddhism.

As students first encounter another religion they may be tempted to focus solely on similarity, to lift up and hang onto ideas, terms, practices, or symbols that seem familiar—just like *x*. This is a perfectly understandable reaction, but it represents the sort of "magical" comparison criticized by Jonathan Z. Smith. While some students may pull back from the strangeness of the other religion, others may rush to imagine themselves as Buddhists. Geertz alerts us to have all students engage the distinctive terms, symbols, institutions, and practices of the other religion—the ways in which the religion represents itself. Students often resist the strange terms and symbols, but it is precisely in wrestling with the strangeness that understanding will begin to emerge; they need to engage the language of the other community before they can develop what Bruffee would call their transitional languages and linguistic flexibility in negotiating broader communities. Flood also considers this negotiation and suggests that understanding is developed in mutually critical conversation with voices, texts, or narratives of the other religion so that students can engage and gradually narrow the gap between their world and the world of the other religion.

Clarity about what aspects of religion can actually be studied also has substantial ramifications for the classroom. Many students are fascinated by the sacred (or Brahman, or the Dao), by enlightenment, mystical states, or religious experience. Such topics are, of course, central to the study of other religions, but teachers and learners need always to keep in mind that they can only access what people say, write, make, or do about or in response to the sacred or religious experience.

Finally, the response to the "posts" has had its impacts on the teaching and learning of religions. It has inspired teachers to invite more spokespersons from the religions into the classroom or to include visits to religious sites as part of learning. It has encouraged the use of novels, books, and films by adherents of traditions to ensure that many voices of the tradition are engaged in depth. It has encouraged attention to women's voices and contemporary voices rather than simply to the classics of traditions. It has made teachers less comfortable with offering comprehensive frameworks and schema for interpreting religions, although learners often still ask for such frameworks. It has encouraged teachers to attend to issues of power and justice in both the history of religions and in their contemporary relationships.

LEARNING RELIGIONS AND LEARNING THEORY

The discussion in this chapter has extended the principles of learning theory discussed in the last chapter into the field of learning religions; the various issues and principles raised dovetail and inform each other.

The diverse ways of learning discussed by Howard Gardner and Mary Field Belenky's team resonate with the diverse voices and perspectives that must be recognized and engaged in another religion. Not only do learners bring their diverse voices, experiences, and human particularities, but they encounter diverse voices, experiences, and particularities in those whom they engage from other religions.

The empowerment of voice and agency advocated by Freire and hooks resonates with the respect for the voices, subjectivities, and agencies of persons from other religions advocated by contemporary scholars of religion. As learners are being encouraged to develop their voices and new patterns of effective behavior, they are also respecting the voices and the agency of those whom they engage in the learning process.

Greene's ideas of broadening horizons and entering other worlds through imagination by means of conversation, art, and narrative resonate with the dialogical approach to the study of religion through mutual critical conversation with persons or narratives articulated by Flood and others. Only through such conversation and engagement of narratives can the gap of difference be gradually and partially bridged.

Bruffee's notion of learning through collaborative conversation helps articulate how the dialogical process articulated by Flood and others might play out in the classroom.

If we seek to interweave the principles discussed in this chapter with those that concluded the previous chapter, we might have something like the following. Learning other religions in a diverse world entails:

1. Building on the diversity of learners' experiences while respecting the internal diversity and multiple perspectives of religions studied

2. Empowering learners by developing voice and agency while also teaching them to respect the voices and agencies of those whom they engage in study

3. Entering other worlds through art, text, or narrative so that learners engage difference and particularity while acknowledging their own and others' social locations

4. Engaging understanding and interpretation of the distinctive ways in which religions represent themselves, and not merely the mastery of ungrounded information

5. Developing linguistic flexibility through a mutually critical conversation that engages the languages of all participants, including those of the religions studied

6. Establishing mutually respectful relationships, learning to stand with others

Though a bit cumbersome, these six principles will be important in learning other religions. However, before we can articulate the threads of the learning process we need to explore aspects of theological learning: What is at stake for Christians learning other religions?

4

Theological Learning

The previous two chapters have discussed teaching and learning theory and issues in the study of religions. This chapter turns more directly to the heart of this project—theological learning. For the purposes of this book, theological learning is defined very broadly as Christian learning either for the sake of leadership in the church or for full and informed participation in Christian life.[1]

Theological learning has a long history, stretching back to the early centuries of the Christian church, but the contemporary situation and understandings of theology and theological learning were shaped by developments in European and American history. This chapter begins with a brief discussion of the historical forces shaping theological learning, and then explores how theological scholars are seeking to redefine the goals and nature of theological learning. The chapter continues with an examination of theological learning and other religions and concludes by articulating some of the theological dimensions that must be addressed in the process of Christians learning other religions.

HISTORICAL CONTEXT:
FORCES THAT HAVE SHAPED THEOLOGICAL LEARNING

For many centuries theological learning consisted of theological reflection on the church's teachings, its interpretations of the Bible, and reflections of scholastic theologians who had systematized such knowledge. At the time of the Reformation, Protestants revised theological learning, grounding it first and foremost in the Bible, which was used to critique and reinterpret the tradition. Protestant theology was based in biblical exegesis. From the base of biblical studies, Protes-

---

[1] There are certainly Jewish, Muslim, Buddhist, and Hindu forms of learning that are in many ways analogous to Christian theological learning. However, Christian theological learning is shaped by a particular history and by the historical and contemporary position of Christianity in North American culture. I therefore limit my discussion in this volume to Christian theological learning, and I invite my colleagues from other religions to consider how and whether any of the ideas addressed in this book pertain to their situation. Our society would certainly benefit from a conversation about many forms of religious learning and how they might constructively interact with and engage one another.

tant students learned dogmatics and history of doctrine "with an eye toward the vindication of the Protestant movement against Roman Catholic claims." Students also prepared for the pastoral office, "translating the scriptural patterns of church leadership and scriptural wisdom concerning its exercise into the contemporary setting."[2] Everything flowed from the scriptural base, which was understood as the normative foundation of tradition.

The fourfold organization of theological learning into biblical, dogmatic/systematic, historical, and practical has dominated theological learning from early Protestant times into our day. Even most Roman Catholic schools follow a similar model, with systematics divided between systematic and moral theology—hence: Bible, historical theology, systematic theology, moral theology, and pastoral theology.[3] Although there have been significant challenges to separate divisions of theological learning, the historical pattern retains its dominance.

By the seventeenth and eighteenth centuries, changes in church leadership and in the disciplines had put considerable strain on the traditional understanding of theological learning. Biblical studies and historical studies were significantly transformed by the rise and dominance of critical historical methodologies. While resisted in many quarters, these methods were ultimately effective in significantly transforming the ways in which scholars and students worked, and in undermining traditional claims about authorship and historical reliability. As these new "scientific" methodologies became prominent, they helped to transform the universities, especially in Germany, into research universities. The theological disciplines of biblical studies, history, and theology were invited into the universities, but a condition of their participation was "to face the challenges posed by modern secular studies."[4]

The shift to critical historical studies fundamentally challenged the traditional approach to the Bible as the Word of God. The Bible was now viewed as a set of historical documents studied by means of historical methods. It was no longer the source of a normative view of history, but was a part of history, subject to historical study. Theology also underwent a transformation in this intellectual context. Whereas in earlier times theology had occasionally drawn on philosophy to help make Christian claims intelligible, now theologians often undertook a thoroughgoing attempt to reconcile Christian belief with one or another philosophical worldview. The burden was now on the theologians to demonstrate that the Christian worldview could stand up to the standards of philosophy. The pastoral or practical dimensions of theological study—preaching, liturgy, pastoral care—also came under scrutiny, primarily because they were deemed insufficiently scientific to be admitted as university disciplines; they were viewed as applications of knowledge rather than as scientific producers of knowledge.[5] This had the dual

---

[2] Charles M. Wood, *Vision and Discernment: An Orientation in Theological Study* (Atlanta: Scholars Press, 1985), 2. My summary of the historical context is based on Wood's lucid account.

[3] I thank James Bretzke for this clarification of the pattern of Roman Catholic theological curricula (personal communication, June 6, 2002).

[4] Wood, *Vision and Discernment*, 5.

[5] Ibid., 7.

impact of marginalizing practical studies (leaving them more in the hands of the churches than the university) and also of cutting off their three partners (biblical studies, theology, and history) from their previously organic ties to the practical in the preparation of students for pastoral leadership.

The separation of scientific from practical in the German research universities was replicated in the structure of American universities. First, there was the division between the core disciplines of the university (arts and sciences) and the practical or professional schools. Later, the establishment of religious studies in American universities further exacerbated the division between the theoretical disciplines of biblical studies, history, and theology/philosophy from the practical disciplines. Since scholars in the theoretical disciplines were increasingly trained in the universities, and since the university guilds increasingly dominated the standards of scholarship and publication, the gap widened between the theoretical and practical disciplines of theological learning.

The theological school today tends to be characterized by a three-stage process of theological learning: historical, including biblical studies; systematic theology; and then practical. The assumption is that the historical and biblical courses provide the data or content of Christian tradition, which is then reflected upon theologically to prepare the learner to adapt or appropriate tradition for the contemporary context.[6] Contemporary critics charge that the three-stage approach both misunderstands the task of theological learning and does a serious injustice to it.

The sharp divide between theoretical and practical disciplines outlined above produced pastors and church leaders who were often unable to relate their "book knowledge" to the practical demands of ministry and leadership. Churches and denominations became sharply critical of what they saw as the failures of theological education, and they tended to demand ever more attention to the practical skills of ministry. What they needed were not scholars, they argued, but skilled practitioners.

Theological educators found themselves caught between the church and the university, fending off critics from both sides. In recent decades, theological scholars have sought to rearticulate the nature and goals of theological education to steer a course between excessive dominance by the scientific models of the research university and the demands for skills-based theological education from the churches.

RETHINKING THE NATURE AND GOALS
OF THEOLOGICAL EDUCATION

Edward Farley sees theology as the Christian community's response to issues, both inside and outside of the church, demanding reflection and action. These issues require reinterpretations of Christian history and teaching for the present

---

[6] Ibid., 16, 62.

context. Thus, theological learning is more fundamentally hermeneutical than scientific. What is needed is "a shift from theology as a cluster of sciences . . . to theology as historically situated reflection and interpretation. The outcome of that shift is that the structure of theological study or pedagogy is recognized to be determined by basic modes of interpretation rather than by sciences."[7] Farley argues for the liberation of theology from so-called objective and scientific approaches rooted in the eighteenth-century German research university and for a turn to interpretation and understanding, a turn that has had significant advocates across the human sciences, from literature to anthropology, from linguistics to history. It also reflects a turn from learning as the inculcation of information to learning as understanding, which we discussed in chapter 2.

Farley also seeks to address the split between theoretical disciplines and pastoral skills. Theological education, he argues, is primarily neither about objective knowledge nor about practical skills, but consists rather in the formation of a disposition or aptitude, which he called a *habitus*. The formation of *habitus* entails both cognitive understanding and patterns of relationship and behavior. This *habitus* is, in Farley's phrase, a "sapiential and personal knowledge."[8] Sapiential knowledge is personal, but it is not individual, for it consists of discerning and developing the dispositions or aptitudes appropriate for effective life in Christian community. Thus the personal wisdom of theological learning is always in and for the sake of Christian community life in the context of the world.

David Kelsey develops Farley's notion of theology as sapiential wisdom, arguing against the skills-based approach to theological education. Kelsey notes the tension between the nonutilitarian aim of theological learning (to understand God truly) and the focus on leadership training as the unifying aim of many theological schools. He articulates the paradox: "It is precisely by being schooled in a way that is governed by an apparently nonutilitarian . . . overarching goal (that is, to understand God simply for the sake of understanding God) that persons can best be prepared to provide church leadership." Church leadership, he argues, is not a set of skills, but leadership based on "wisdom rooted in faith, hope, and love of God."[9] Thus, for Kelsey, theological education is best designed not according to the model of the modern research university, which he calls the Berlin model, but rather according to the ancient Greek model of *paideia*, the nurturance of the person and formation of wisdom, which he calls the Athens model.[10] Kelsey's wisdom model of theological education focuses on the development of Christian character.

---

[7] Edward Farley, *The Fragility of Knowledge: Theological Education in the Church and the University* (Philadelphia: Fortress Press, 1988), 128.

[8] Edward Farley, *Theologia: The Fragmentation and Unity of Theological Education* (Philadelphia: Fortress Press, 1983), xi.

[9] David H. Kelsey, *To Understand God Truly: What's Theological about a Theological School?* (Louisville: Westminster John Knox Press, 1992), 245, 248.

[10] David H. Kelsey, *Between Athens and Berlin: The Theological Education Debate* (Grand Rapids: Wm. B. Eerdmans, 1993).

If Kelsey develops another version of wisdom-based theological education, Charles Wood aspires to redefine and thus transcend its apparent tension between theory and practice. He writes,

> The conventional and centuries-old division of the theological disciplines into the theoretical and the practical is seriously misleading. It implicitly denies the properly theoretical aspects of practical theology, and it exaggerates the extent to which the other disciplines are themselves theoretical enterprises. However, the division does not merely misrepresent reality; it also transforms it after its own image. That is, when the division is embodied in patterns of theological inquiry and education, when the disciplinary and curricular structure of theology assumes its validity, it becomes self-fulfilling.[11]

Wood argues that theory and practice cannot be neatly separated, nor can they properly be seen as the sequential stages in the Protestant version of theological education as beginning with history, followed by systematic theological reflection, which then sets the stage for theologically informed practice. To replace the theory-versus-practice distinction, Wood proposes instead a distinction between vision (a general synoptic understanding and overview of the Christian tradition) and discernment (insight into particular contexts). Although these appear at first to be opposed, they are actually dialectically related and require each other. Wood notes that while necessary in Christian witness, vision is also fraught with dangers: of theological distortion, as our views are always unconsciously shaped by our circumstances; of mistakenly ascribing universality to our vision; of misrepresentation in the act of construing our vision; and of the temptation to gloss over ambiguity and tragedy.[12] In articulating the dangers of a synoptic vision of the Christian tradition, Wood is acknowledging the historical groundedness and particularity of every Christian and Christian community; every Christian has access to only a portion of the vast cumulative tradition.[13]

   The corrective to the dangers inherent in any vision, Wood argues, is discernment: close attention to particular contexts, actions, and events. Both vision (synoptic overview) and discernment (attention to context) are theoretical and practical at the same time; theory and practice constantly inform and critique each other. Theological learning always addresses the validity of Christian witness in both historical and contemporary contexts. For Wood, understanding of tradition (vision) and reappropriation of tradition in light of particular circumstances (discernment) develop together. It is not a matter of getting the theological understanding of tradition right before the Christian seeks to act in a particular context, but a dialectical back-and-forth movement between the Chris-

---

[11] Wood, *Vision and Discernment*, 67.

[12] Ibid., 72.

[13] See the discussion of historical particularity and of Wilfred Cantwell Smith's cumulative tradition in chapter 3.

tian's sense of tradition in relationship to particular contexts, and by extension to new learnings and understanding.

Theological learning, then, entails both the understanding of Christian tradition and its reappropriation in light of present circumstances. It is a hermeneutical or interpretive field, not a "scientific" field. Its goal is focused on the development of Christian understandings, aptitudes, dispositions, and character so that the Christian learner can reappropriate the tradition in light of contemporary circumstances. Theological learning provides the Christian's self-understanding and ability to live faithfully within the Christian community and in relationship to the broader world. But what happens when that "broader world" includes the presence of other religions?

THEOLOGICAL LEARNING AND OTHER RELIGIONS

Until relatively recently those engaged in Christian theology and theological education ignored the presence of other religions as irrelevant to theological learning. The Christian tradition, this view held, was shaped by a divine revelation of the gospel; only the special revelation of Jesus Christ presented in the Bible offered a window on divine truth. This view was well represented in Hendrik Kraemer's *Christian Message in a Non-Christian World*.[14] Kraemer's book had a powerful impact on many Christians in the Asian world, causing them to break off all conversations with the other religions among which they lived. They had nothing whatever to do with the traditions of their ancestors, fearing that any such involvement would compromise their Christian faith.[15] Asian Christians and Asian Christian leaders, then, were held back from adapting Christian beliefs and practices to their own cultural contexts. There was a need to indigenize Christianity, exploring how it might be expressed through local symbols, and to contextualize it, exploring what the gospel is and means in Asian contexts.[16] In Europe and America, where Christianity was the culturally dominant religion, books like Kraemer's kept many theological educators from engaging, or even recognizing, the increasing religious diversity of Christian lives.

In another corner of the theological world, Christians began from the end of the nineteenth century to engage in dialogue with representatives of other religions. In 1893 the World's Parliament of Religions was convened in Chicago in conjunction with the World's Fair. Several of the liberal Protestant scholars of religion, including Max Müller, supported the Parliament and participated in it. The Parliament brought religious leaders from around the world to discuss their

---

[14] Hendrik Kraemer, *The Christian Message in a Non-Christian World* (New York: Harper, for the International Missionary Council, 1938.)

[15] S. Wesley Ariarajah, "Christian Minorities Amidst Other Faith Traditions," *Ecumenical Review* 41, no. 1 (January 1989): 24-26. Ariajah notes that Kraemer was unhappy with the impact of his book and, in his later writings, was clearer about the values of other traditions (p. 22).

[16] Ibid., 27-28.

traditions and to enter into dialogue about the unity of the world's religions. Dialogues continued beyond the Parliament, coalescing after World War I around the issue of world religions uniting to promote world peace.[17] This movement is well represented by Sarvepalli Radhakrishnan, a Hindu Brahmin, who twice held professorships in comparative or Eastern religions at Oxford University before returning to India for a career in politics. Radhakrishnan was a rigorous scholar of comparative religion; he believed that the scientific study of religion must "treat all religions in a spirit of absolute detachment and impartiality."[18] However, he also held that the study of comparative religion will reveal religion as a universal phenomenon, and he urged the religions to mutual understanding. He wrote,

> The keynote of the new attitude is expressed by the word "sharing." The different religious men of the East and the West are to share their visions and insights, hopes and fears, plans and purposes. Unhappily, just as in the political region, so here also this is more an aspiration than an actuality. Comparative Religion helps us to further this ideal of the sharing among religions which no longer stand in uncontaminated isolation. . . . They are fellow workers toward the same goal.[19]

The centennial of the World's Parliament was convened in Chicago in 1993 and issued a document calling for a global ethic.[20] However inspiring these vast assemblies may be, it is exceedingly difficult to affirm a single goal, particularly if participants seek to honor the particular values and understandings of the religions and not impose the language, values, and visions of one or two globally dominant religions.

The challenges of developing understanding across the lines of different religions are perhaps best addressed in bilateral interreligious dialogue, and many theologians and educated Christians have participated in such dialogues. Dialogical courses are occasionally part of the theological curriculum, but they are more often a part of the lives or ongoing education of Christian leaders, lay and ordained.

Serious bilateral dialogue, if its goal is genuine understanding, profoundly engages difference and constrains any rush to identify similarities. For example, David Tracy has noted that despite several decades of engagement by brilliant and well-intentioned participants, Buddhist–Christian dialogue has in large part clarified profound senses of difference. He writes, "A more 'other' form of

---

[17] Eric J. Sharpe, *Comprarative Religion: A History,* 2nd ed. (Chicago: Open Court Publishing, 1986), chapter 11.

[18] S. Radhakrishnan, *East and West in Religion* (London: G. Allen and Unwin, 1933), 16, cited in Sharpe, *Comparative Religion,* 259.

[19] Radhakrishnan, *East and West in Religion,* 26, cited in Sharpe, *Comparative Religion,* 259.

[20] Hans Küng and Karl-Josef Kuschel, eds., *A Global Ethic: The Declaration of the Parliament of the World's Religions* (New York: Continuum, 1993).

thought than Buddhist thought on God and self, on history and nature, indeed, on thought itself (including dialogical thought) would be difficult to conceive for Western Christians without different strategies and categories of philosophical and theological thought."[21] The task of understanding such a different religion requires a thoughtful hermeneutical strategy, an approach to developing understanding gradually, through the careful and mutually critical give-and-take of conversation.[22] The road to understanding winds through a spectrum of mutual responses, including the identification not of similarities but of similarities-in-difference. As we come to understand the other, we come to understand differently (to be transformed), and to see some "suggestive possibility" in what we learn from the other.[23] These "suggestive possibilities" from other religions in turn enrich our Christian theological understandings.

Sometimes, however, what we learn of another religion is not a possibility for us, even if we can grasp it as a human possibility for the other. Lee Yearley has called this response "spiritual regret."[24] Spiritual regret recognizes that a broad range of legitimate religious ideals exist, but that no one person can exhibit all of them. We may comprehend and honor a belief or practice of another religion as having value for its adherents but remain unable to adopt it as our own.

Francis Schüssler Fiorenza believes that the very task of Christian theologizing always occurs within the context of religious diversity. He writes,

> Theology seeks to specify the ideal potentials and paradigms of identity within its tradition. It seeks to consider the demands of diverse practices. It seeks to reflect on appropriate background theories of contemporary worldviews. Theology seeks to achieve this reflective equilibrium within a community of discourse that is in conversation with other communities of discourse, representing distinct traditions of religious and social practice.[25]

Like Tracy, Fiorenza acknowledges the challenges and difficulties of understanding and engaging another religion or culture, but he puts the challenge in Wittgensteinian terms. "These diverse forms of faith exist, in Wittgenstein's terminology, as 'forms of life' with diverse shared practices, customs, and institutions. . . . How is understanding of other religions possible when one does not

---

[21] David Tracy, *Dialogue with the Other: The Inter-Religious Dialogue*, Louvain Theological and Pastoral Monographs 1 (Grand Rapids: Wm. B. Eerdmans, 1991), 69.

[22] Tracy's understanding of hermeneutics through conversation is built on Hans-Georg Gadamer, Jürgen Habermas, Paul Ricoeur, and Mircea Eliade.

[23] Ibid., 40, 42-44.

[24] Lee H. Yearley, "New Religious Virtues and the Study of Religion," Fifteenth Annual University Lecture in Religion, Arizona State University, February 10, 1994, 5, http://www.asu.edu/clas/religious_studies/home/1994lec.html.

[25] Francis Schüssler Fiorenza, "Theological and Religious Studies: The Contest of the Faculties," in *Shifting Boundaries: Contextual Approaches to the Structure of Theological Education,* ed. Barbara G. Wheeler and Edward Farley (Louisville: Westminster John Knox Press, 1991), 140.

share the practices, customs, and institutions of those beliefs?"[26] The problems of interpreting other religions are vexing and have led some to argue that we can never understand another religion because it is simply too different from our own experience. However, Fiorenza believes that shared problems of human experience (e.g., peace, ecological issues, etc.) cut across cultural and religious lines, even if they are understood differently. These shared human issues offer a common ground from which conversation across lines of difference can begin.

In the contemporary theological world, there are strong advocates for contextualized theologies and for sophisticated and responsible forms of interreligious dialogue. The issue remains, however, of whether and how these or other means of addressing religious pluralism are addressed in theological education. In general, most would agree, theological education remains largely monoreligious.

Paul Knitter has been a courageous if somewhat lonely voice arguing for the necessity of moving beyond a monoreligious theological education. Knitter, the author of a series of influential volumes on the relationship of Christianity to other faiths, is convinced that part of the failure of theological education is because

[t]heological educators are going about their job of reflecting and reconstructing on the basis of an exclusive, or too restrictive, use of Christian tradition and experience. They are not able effectively and engagingly to reflect on and reconstruct Christian tradition and identity because they have closed themselves to, or are not sufficiently open to, other religious traditions and identities.[27]

He suggests that a major factor in this failure is Christians' fear of losing their privileged position: "Christian theological education today is ailing because it has locked itself within—or is fearful of stepping outside of—the house of its own aggrandized and isolated authority."[28]

This fear and isolation have serious consequences because the reality of religious diversity is a fact of Christian lives. Knitter believes that this diversity calls Christians to engage other religions in conversation. Such a call has profound implications for how we think about theological learning. In the first place, it significantly broadens and redefines the view of tradition. Knitter writes,

Our conversational awareness of other religions enables us to repossess the traditional Christian assertion that God is a power of universal and self-communicating love and that therefore there is a universal revelatory presence of God within all creation. . . . If we believe that God has spoken to

---

[26] Ibid., 134.

[27] Paul F. Knitter, "Beyond a Mono-religious Theological Education," in *Shifting Boundaries*, ed. Wheeler and Farley, 151.

[28] Ibid., 153.

others, we must enter into a conversation with that Word. To affirm only Christian tradition as the source or sole norm for divine revelation is to disrespect what God has revealed elsewhere. The Christian Word is incomplete without other Words.[29]

Knitter makes a theological argument for a strong Christian pluralist position.[30] Although many have not yet reached the point where they are prepared to affirm so strong a pluralist argument, Knitter challenges his fellow Christians to take seriously the theological implications of their acceptance of the reality of religious pluralism.

Knitter plays out the implications of his position for theological learning. Building on Fiorenza's notions that texts are interpreted in light of their life practices, Knitter suggests,

> [W]e cannot understand the meaning and truth of our religious classics unless we also analyze and evaluate the life-practices that they produce— including those practices that affect, positively and negatively, other religious communities and their classics. And we will be able truly to comprehend such practices only if we hear directly from those religious communities.[31]

For Knitter, both biblical studies and the studies of great thinkers of the Christian tradition are appropriately studied in dialogue with persons of other communities who can speak to how Christian texts, and the practices arising from them, have affected the lives of their own religious communities.

Like Fiorenza, Knitter believes that issues of justice can open a common ground for conversation, but he cautions that in addressing issues of justice we must be aware of the history of domination and oppression. Not every participant in the conversation has the same relationship to each practical justice issue, and the effects of long patterns of domination and oppression are difficult to unravel —yet this is essential work. In Knitter's view, then, conversation also entails a commitment to the liberation and freedom of all partners to the conversation so that they can participate as equals. For him oppression is not an abstraction, but is embedded in patterns of human behavior; as individuals engaged in conversation, we must seek to change our own behavior in ways that will undercut patterns of injustice.[32]

---

[29] Ibid., 161.

[30] My Buddhist colleague Richard Payne reminds me that Knitter's pluralism, while strongly pluralistic, is still Christian-centric in that it defines other religions in Christian terms as God's revelations. From outside of Christianity, this can appear as a more sophisticated form of triumphalism. Richard's response underscores the challenge for Christians in finding a Christian position of pluralism that transcends triumphalist assumptions (personal communication, May 29, 2002).

[31] Knitter, "Beyond a Mono-religious Theological Eduation," 162.

[32] Ibid., 169.

David Tracy, Francis Schüssler Fiorenza, and Paul Knitter are theologians reflecting on theological learning and theological education in the context of religious pluralism. They are in the process of articulating a stance for Christians who seek some mode of engagement with other religious views. Their views are far from dominant among Christians today, but they need to be heard, debated, and refined.

If Tracy, Fiorenza, and Knitter address this issue from the standpoint of theologians, religious educators have also discussed theological learning in relation to other religions. A number of religious educators contributed essays to a volume entitled *Religious Pluralism and Religious Education*.[33] The volume's editor, Norma Thompson, sees theological learning as expanding Christian relationships. She writes that "education is more than transmitting a heritage; it is learning, living, and growing within a community which must relate to larger and larger communities until it encompasses the entire world."[34] For Thompson, a major aspect of theological learning is the building of relationships, both within one's own community and with those of other communities. Constance Tarasar notes, "More than *knowledge about* the other, we need *knowledge of* those who are different from us. We need to try to experience, to whatever extent possible, their tradition—their vision and their way of life."[35] James Michael Lee writes, "If we are to teach learners to engage in religiously pluralistic activities, we should teach them how to love other religious traditions and their adherents rather than simply to know them."[36]

These authors express a strong Christian desire to establish positive relations with members of other communities. My Buddhist colleague Richard Payne reminds me that others may not always wish to engage in relationships with Christians. It is easy to assume that our willingness to enter relationships will always automatically be reciprocated. Matters are not so simple. Sometimes we need humility and patience to discern when and under what conditions our overtures would be welcome and appropriate.[37]

Lee offers his case for the necessity of Christian learning embracing religious pluralism. First, other religions are simply there; they are a fact of our existence. Second, such engagement enables us to appreciate more profoundly and to live more deeply our own form of religion. Third, engagement with other religions helps us to correct and transform our own religion so that it can move into the future, becoming what it is meant to be. Fourth, engagement with other religions

---

[33] Norma H. Thompson, ed., *Religious Pluralism and Religious Education* (Birmingham, Ala.: Religious Education Press, 1988).

[34] Norma H. Thompson, "The Challenge of Religious Pluralism," in *Religious Pluralism and Religious Education*, ed. Thompson, 19.

[35] Constance J. Tarasar, "The Minority Problem: Educating for Identity and Openness," in *Religious Pluralism and Religious Education*, ed. Thompson, 205-6 (italics in original).

[36] James Michael Lee, "The Blessings of Religious Pluralism," in *Religious Pluralism and Religious Education*, ed. Thompson, 71.

[37] Personal communication, May 29, 2002.

allows us to bring the fruits of our tradition to those from other traditions. Many Christians hope not only to learn from, but to share in such encounters.[38]

Lee's position is a clear Christian statement. All points but the first are cast in terms of benefits to Christians; they are to be enriched, to correct, transform, and strengthen Christianity, and to bring Christian witness to others. While Lee recognizes that Christians' views will be corrected and transformed by the experience, the pluralistic learning he proposes is seen entirely from a Christian viewpoint and agenda. It is important to recognize that adherents of other religions may be put off by this agenda. While in some situations mutual sharing will be welcomed, for example, in others Christian sharing can be seen as a reversion to aggressive Christian witness with the purpose of conversion. The legacy of the history of Christian mission can make some conversations difficult. If Knitter's proposal, above, may be more pluralistic than many Christians can affirm, Lee's proposal may be off-putting to non-Christian conversation partners. This is a delicate balance.

Finally, while not directly pertinent to theological learning of other religions, I want to note that theological educators have developed experientially based liberationist models of theological learning that are well suited to address difference and pluralism in all of its forms. An interesting example is Rebecca Chopp's *Saving Work*. Chopp seeks "to develop a new method of reflection on theological education that attended to cultural movements and actual practices within theological education, based on the current subjects (the students) of theological education."[39] Her approach empowers women to develop the narratives of their lives as the subject of theological education, and from there to develop new practices of Christian community and of Christian conversation. The experientially based narrative approach attends to human difference and uses conversation to forge both new understandings and new patterns of relationship and behavior.

Mary Boys developed a similar model of engaged pedagogy, articulating "modes of teaching congruent with feminist and other liberation perspectives that seek to engage course participants in critical discourses that will have a transformative effect on society."[40] Her article explores how to create engaged dialogue in collaborative learning communities that can hone the critical thinking of learners. She offers rules and principles for dialogical pedagogy, noting that "[d]ialogue is not . . . a mere method. *It is a way of life*, and, as such calls for attentiveness to the emotions, virtues, and skills that nurture relationship."[41]

Neither Chopp nor Boys directly addresses Christians learning other religions, but their pedagogical approaches build from the experiences of students, and both

---

[38] Lee, "Blessings of Religious Pluralism," 59-63.

[39] Rebecca S. Chopp, *Saving Work: Feminist Practices of Theological Education* (Louisville: Westminster John Knox Press, 1995), x.

[40] Mary C. Boys, "Engaged Pedagogy: Dialogue and Critical Reflection," *Teaching Theology and Religion* 2, no. 3 (October 1999): 129.

[41] Ibid., 133 (italics in original).

develop the sort of critical conversation and dialogical skills entailed in such learning.

THEOLOGICAL LEARNING AND LEARNING RELIGIONS

The authors in this chapter highlight a tension that some might see as a contradiction between two tasks of theological learning. One is the appropriation and reappropriation of Christian tradition, while the other is preparing Christians to live as a community among the other communities in our diverse world. The first seems to many (and, most importantly, to theological learners themselves) to require a sort of isolation, a focus on Christian tradition and community so that believers can locate and understand themselves *as Christians*. This desire for knowledge of the tradition is exacerbated by the fact that many in the churches and even in theological schools have not been "traditioned" from birth, steeped in the traditions of a single denomination. Many Christians, and even seminarians, have had complex religious lives—in and out of many denominations of the church, or of two or more religions. The second demand of theological education to relate as Christians to the broader community seems a vast and sometimes overwhelming enterprise—to learn about the various cultures and religions of the world, to understand the complex histories and circumstances of the many others with whom we relate as Christians.

Although these two goals of theological learning often seem to pull in different directions, they are in fact related, as an analogy to human self-identity and human relatedness suggests. On the one hand, a human being with an inadequate sense of self cannot enter successfully into relationships with others, as he has no sense of what he is bringing to the relationship. So a Christian with no sense of Christian identity has no base from which to enter into relationships with others; there is, as Gertrude Stein said of Oakland, California, "no there there." On the other hand, a person with a rigid sense of identity also cannot enter into relations with others, as he is too closed off and closed down to negotiate the relationship. In the same way, an overly rigid and fearful sense of Christian identity closes off relationships that could enrich both Christians and the adherents of other religions. Relationships may or may not be successful or fruitful; they may end in more disagreement than agreement. But not to enter them at all closes off any possibility of mutual understanding.

Some theological learners may also fear that engaging other religions will threaten their hard-won sense of Christian identity. Such fear is not unique to religion: understanding across lines of difference raises issues of discomfort that the world will not be what it has been. Clifford Geertz, one of the most articulate interpreters of crosscultural experience, writes,

Whatever use the imaginative productions of other peoples . . . can have for our moral lives, then, it cannot be to simplify them. The image of the past (or the primitive, or the classic, or the exotic) as a source of remedial wisdom, a prosthetic corrective for a damaged spiritual life—an image that has governed a good deal of humanist thought and education—is mischievous because it leads us to expect that our uncertainties will be reduced by access to thought-worlds constructed along lines alternative to our own, when in fact they will be multiplied. . . . [T]he growth in range a powerful sensibility gains from an encounter with another one, as powerful or more, comes only at the expense of its inward ease.[42]

Although we may benefit from our knowledge of and engagement with other cultures and religions, such knowledge will not be easy or comfortable. There is always some loss of inward ease, an overturning of comfortable assumptions and cherished truths, or, on the other hand, the discovery that we do not think much of the other religion after all.

Engagements across lines of religious or cultural difference always entail both a passing over and a coming back.[43] On coming back, we must determine, "What do I make of what I have been made?" In other words, has the crossing over into another religious world confirmed our prior experiences and values, or has it lifted up issues that seem wrong, that need to be addressed, within one's home community, for example, issues of justice or bigotry? William Pinar comments, "One must then work against this particular legacy, perhaps through logic, perhaps through prayer and other religious means, perhaps through study."[44] Pinar's remarks clarify what James Michael Lee means when he says that engagement with religious others will help correct and transform one's community. One aspect of those engagements may be to reaffirm the central convictions of Christian identity; another may be to highlight narrow or distorted views that require prayerful reconsideration for a corrected view of gospel teaching.

There is one way in which the tension between the two goals (appropriating and reappropriating Christian tradition versus helping Christians to engage in dialogue with other communities) raises a delicate issue for theological learning. As Diana Eck notes, "For those of us who teach religion, the multireligious classroom environment makes vividly clear that there *is* no presumptive normative viewpoint; the language of the 'other' is no longer acceptable, for we are all other to one another."[45] Eck's description of the multireligious classroom creates the possibility of dialogue among many positions where no one religion becomes the

---

[42] Clifford Geertz, *Local Knowledge: Further Essays in Interpretive Anthropology*, 2nd ed. (New York: Basic Books, 2000), 44-45.

[43] John S. Dunne, *The Way of all the Earth: Experiments in Truth and Religion* (New York: Macmillan, 1972), ix. I thank Philip Wickeri for bringing Dunne to my attention (personal communication, June 10, 2002).

[44] William F. Pinar, *Autobiography, Politics, and Sexuality: Essays in Curriculum Theory, 1972-1992* (New York: Peter Lang, 1994), 204.

[45] Diana L. Eck, "Dialogue and Method: Reconstructing the Study of Religion," in *A Magic Still Dwells: Comparative Religion in the Postmodern Age,* ed. Kimberley C. Patton and Benjamin C. Ray (Berkeley: University of California Press, 2000), 133-34.

standard for the others, or against which others are compared. This is harder to achieve in the theological classroom, as that environment very seldom has multireligious balance. The dominance of Christianity in the theological classroom must be considered and addressed if genuine dialogue and conversation are to occur.

Many of the general principles of theological learning resonate with the learning principles discussed in previous chapters. Chopp's experientially based feminist learning developed from narratives of women's lives resonates with the first three principles discussed in the last two chapters: (1) building on the diversity of learners' experiences, (2) empowering learners by developing their voice and agency; and (3) entering other worlds, through arts, text, or narrative. The hermeneutical approaches to learning developed by Farley, Tracy, and Fiorenza resonate with the last three principles of learning: (4) engaging understanding and interpretation of the distinctive ways in which religions represent themselves; (5) developing linguistic flexibility through mutually critical conversation; (6) establishing mutually respectful relationships, learning to stand with others. Mary Boys's engaged dialogical pedagogy resonates well with all six principles.

What makes theological learning distinctive is its development of Christian character, *habitus*, or wisdom, the deepening of Christian understanding and of Christian lives. As the theological learner learns more about the context of her Christian life—including the impact of religious diversity in it—that learning is folded back into her reappropriation of what it means to be Christian, her sense of the Christian tradition and its language of self-understanding. Thus the theological learner does not merely learn other religions, but reappropriates her learnings into Christian reflection and self-understanding, as "suggestive possibilities" or "spiritual regret" or in some other form.

The important tension and balance between learning another religion well (as articulated by the field of the study of religions) and between theological reflection on that learning (necessitated by theological learning) will frame the threads of the learning process, which will be also deeply informed by the principles of learning discussed in these three chapters. We now turn to the process of Christians learning other religions.

5

Unraveling the Threads

The Process of Learning Another Religion

This chapter articulates what happens when a Christian learns another religion. Unraveling, naming, and describing the threads of the learning process offer one interpretation of that process, written from my specific location (shaped by the particularities of my education and life experience—professional, personal, religious—and also shaped by the reading and research I have done for this book). Assuming that very few others have the opportunity to read deeply in the three areas of my research—learning theory, the study of religions, theological learning—I offer this articulation of the learning process in the hopes of drawing others into a conversation to which they will contribute their expertise and experience.

The learning process is articulated as interpretation, not as an "objective" structure or model. The articulation of these various threads is a device to bring to light several facets of what is admittedly a complex process. Its purpose is to develop a particular form of awareness, an alertness to dimensions of learning that may be overlooked, to the detriment of the learner and, ultimately, of the communities in which the learner participates.

In this process learners (1) enter other worlds through engaging and crossing boundaries of significant difference; (2) begin the task of interpretation and understanding by responding from their distinctive religious locations; (3) enter a series of conversations and dialogues both with the voices of the other tradition and also with other Christians seeking to develop more flexible language for understanding Christian tradition in relation to other religious possibilities; (4) begin to live out new relationships and Christian practices based on the new understandings; and (5) internalize the learning process so that they can continue developing such conversations and relationships. The stages in the process do not always follow in sequence; the various aspects of learning reinforce one another.

Threads of the learning process are held in tension by two poles: (1) understanding another religion faithfully and (2) reappropriating Christian tradition in light of new understandings and relationships. It is difficult, if not impossible, to speak of both of these poles simultaneously; they represent very different dimensions of the learning process. Yet they are not so much contradictory as complementary. The discussion of the threads will articulate both the tensions between these two poles of the learning process and their complementarity.

THREADS OF THE LEARNING PROCESS

1. ENCOUNTERING DIFFERENCE/ENTERING OTHER WORLDS

One of the two major threads of learning another religion is understanding "the other" across areas of difference. Such a statement is commonsensical, but it is no simple matter.

In everyday parlance "different" generally means a new and interesting, or shocking and off-putting, variation of the "same old." "I try to eat a different vegetable every day of the week." "That's a different shade of lipstick!" "Why not try a different flavor of ice cream?" Occasionally it means "odd" or "not the expected": "She has a very different attitude about gift giving." In all of these cases, "difference" is a variation from an accepted norm. The statements presume that there is a generally accepted understanding of the categories: vegetables, lipstick, ice cream, and gift giving.

However, within the theories of understanding and interpretation (hermeneutics), difference is more problematic and is related to statements such as: From a wife to her husband "How can you possibly understand what a woman feels?" From a teenager to his parents, "You'll never understand what it's like for me. Your world is different!" This sort of difference, seen as a barrier to understanding, is created by very different life experiences (based in these examples on gender and generation). The common denominator or category is human life, but that category is too general and nonspecific to be a basis for the understanding demanded by the wife or the teenager.

What these ordinary examples highlight is a central principle of the theory of understanding: that understanding is shaped by what Wittgenstein called "a form of life," a set of experiences and practices that constitute the world of a group or community. Human understanding is always shaped by the interpreter's location and experience, which may be quite different from the location and experience she seeks to understand. Herein lies the challenge of difference, of otherness: we inevitably understand and interpret on the basis of the past experience that has constituted or shaped us, but we are also drawn to understand others shaped by other life experiences. As Francis Schüssler Fiorenza notes, different religions constitute different forms of life "with diverse shared practices, customs, and institutions." He asks, "How is understanding of other religions possible when one does not share the practices, customs, and institutions of those beliefs?"[1]

---

[1] Francis Schüssler Fiorenza, "Theological and Religious Studies: The Contest of the Faculties," in *Shifting Boundaries: Contextual Approaches to the Structure of Theological Education*, ed. Barbara G. Wheeler and Edward Farley (Louisville: Westminster John Knox Press, 1991), 134.

Interpretation of human beings across lines of difference is a challenging task requiring sustained and careful effort.

The first principle in that effort is recognizing and acknowledging difference as difference, not reducing another person, culture, or religion to a variation of what the interpreter knows based on his own "form of life." This principle cannot be overemphasized, since in the interests of making other religions accessible, authors and teachers all too often present them as simply variations on the familiar. They might present another's religion entirely in the terms, structures, and categories familiar to Christians, especially Protestants. Or they may use philosophical and cultural categories that are familiar to their readers. For example in many textbooks and courses, Laozi is presented as the "founder" of Daoism and the *Daodejing* as its "scripture." Such a presentation is highly misleading, a projection of the importance of Jesus and the Gospels in the history of Christianity. As a matter of fact, we are uncertain whether such a figure as Laozi ever existed, and—if he did—whether he authored all or any of the book associated with his name. Moreover, while the *Daodejing* has certainly been influential in Chinese culture, "Daoism" as a religion began with other revelations and scriptures. These later scriptures and their teachings have until recently been ignored or dismissed by Western textbooks as lesser forms of Daoism.

A basic rule of thumb is that if a book is too readable, or a course on other religions too accessible, if it does not stretch or challenge the ways in which learners think about religion and religious practice, then it has not properly introduced the "otherness," the "difference" of the religions. As Clifford Geertz reminded us, "[T]he growth in range a powerful sensibility gains from an encounter with another one, as powerful or more, comes only at the expense of its inward ease."[2] In other words, a genuine encounter with another religion should cause some discomfort, some loss of "inward ease."[3]

The previous three chapters have articulated various aspects and modes of the encounter with difference, as well as strategies to help learners enter into other worlds of meaning and experience. The three basic aims of all of the aspects and strategies of encountering difference are (1) recognizing and acknowledging difference, (2) coming to know others well and accurately, and (3) coming to know others as far as is possible on their own terms. The first principle stands in some tension with the other two, as acknowledgment of difference underscores the challenges of coming to know the other well or on his own terms. Our understanding of others will always be partial and open to correction.[4]

One way of encountering differences is to enter directly and experientially

---

[2] Clifford Geertz, *Local Knowledge: Further Essays in Interpretive Anthropology*, 2nd ed. (New York: Basic Books, 2000), 45.

[3] My colleague Denis Thalson reminds me to underscore that the necessity of facing some discomfort is often resisted by students. Teachers need to be clear and articulate about the necessity and benefits of facing such discomfort (personal communication, May 28, 2002).

[4] I am indebted to Matthew Farris for reminding me of this point (personal communication, June 1, 2002).

into relationships with other people and to experience their beliefs and practices. For instance, a local Taichi instructor may be invited into class to teach students some general principles and movements of Taichi. Or students might attend a local festival in a Daoist temple, asking the participants to explain what it means.

The strategy of direct experience and face-to-face encounter is resonant with Wilfred Cantwell Smith's position that religion is the faith of human beings, lived always in a specific context.[5] From Smith's perspective, religion is studied best not through data or lists of doctrines but in the lives of people shaped by a particular religion. While this is the most adequate way to gain access to religion, Smith reminds us that any given person or group represents and engages only a limited cross-section of a vast cumulative tradition.[6] Thus, it is important to recognize that any direct experience of a religion is particular and limited.

Not every learner will have the opportunity for a sustained direct experience of a religion; in most cases, such direct experiences will constitute a small but vital portion of the learning experience. Even if no such direct experience is possible, there are other ways to "enter" or encounter the different "world" of another religion. An important way—even in direct encounters such as a visit to a temple or religious site—is exposure to the actual voices of the religion. These voices are not singular (there are always different voices, both across history and in contemporary communities), but it is important that learners encounter the distinctive voices and language of the religion, and not solely a description mediated and re-presented through a textbook or interpreter from outside the tradition. That is not to say that the author of a textbook or a Christian with extensive experience of another tradition may not helpfully report what she has learned, but that the reporter must take care to report faithfully and not to obscure the distinctive voices of the other religion, to avoid setting herself up as the representative of another tradition. A textbook or expert should be a bringer of voices and a reporter, not a spokesperson.[7]

Another dimension of attention to the voices of the other religion is to honor a living religion and not to render it a lifeless and voiceless thing. Other threads of the learning process will articulate and develop dialogical and conversational dimensions of learning. For dialogue to be possible, all parties must be heard. Here I stress that giving others an opportunity to speak about their experiences of their religion is an important element of the encounter with difference.

---

[5] Wilfred Cantwell Smith, *Towards a World Theology: Faith and the Comparative History of Religion* (Philadelphia: Westminster Press, 1981; Maryknoll, N.Y.: Orbis Books, 1989), 3.

[6] Ibid., 24-25.

[7] Raymond Williams reminds me that, whatever one's intentions, the reality is not always so simple. Raymond has had his books on Hinduism assigned by Indian swamis for their students (personal communication, May 28, 2002). I know what Raymond means. I have had the strange experience of having my book on the Three-in-One Religion of Lin Chao-en used as a "theological" resource by parties holding a conference to revive the religion in contemporary Fukien. Thus, one can find oneself as the spokesperson for a religion without ever intending to take on that role. The point I am making here, however, is about the role of the teacher in a Western classroom; for me to assume the role of an authoritative interpreter of the Three-in-One religion would be inappropriate; it is my intent to report faithfully what is taught by the textual record.

There is yet another dimension of the other voices, however. Everyday under-standings of conversation, particularly in the United States, characterized by its assumptions of radical individualism, tend to view the voice of another as the voice of a free-floating, disconnected individual. If learners meet members of other religions simply as individuals, they will miss a great deal. Mary Elizabeth Moore warns, "Encountering persons apart from their culture is an extreme of abstraction and individualism; it fosters a tendency, often unconscious, to judge others through our own cultural lenses. In this case, the encounter is superficial, partial, and misleading."[8] Alphonso Lingis eloquently articulates the "forms of life" behind the speech of another person:

> When the other speaks, it is with the tongue of a nation, the intonation of a class, the rhetoric of a social position, the idiom of a subculture, the vocabulary of an age group. . . . One sees behind his feelings the structure of hierarchies, the rites of passage of a culture, the polarities of ideologies. One envisions behind her speech the semantic, syntactic, grammatical, and phonetic patterns of a cultural arena and a history.[9]

As Lingis's description reminds us, in order to listen to and understand the voices of others, we need to be able also to perceive and understand the forces, the "forms of life," that have shaped those voices.

One way to enter the world of meaning shaping the disparate voices and prac-tices of individuals from another religion is to encounter the texts of the religion. These texts were written or edited by—and therefore represent—voices from the religion. They draw the reader into the distinctive language and ideas of the reli-gion, the world of meaning as constructed in texts.[10]

To the extent that they are narratives, the texts also represent themselves as a world of meaning, a reading or retelling of the world. Human beings make mean-ing through narrative; we "inescapably understand our lives in narrative form, as a 'quest.'"[11] Participants in religions also create narratives to tell the story of how and what their religion "means" to them. They not only tell a story, but in doing so they create and refine the particular language and images used to convey the story; the story re-presents the religion in the words and actions of the partici-pants themselves.

Maxine Greene has argued that, because as human beings we all constitute our world through narrative, we are also able to enter into the stories told by others.

---

[8] Mary Elizabeth Mullino Moore, *Teaching from the Heart: Theology and Educational Method,* 2nd ed. (Harrisburg, Penn.: Trinity Press International, 1998), 185.

[9] Alphonso Lingis, *The Community of Those Who have Nothing in Common* (Bloomington: Indi-ana University Press, 1994), 24-25.

[10] Francis X. Clooney, S.J., has developed a process of Christians engaging other religions by a careful and thorough reading of texts (*Seeing Through Texts: Doing Theology Among the Srivais-navas of South India* [Albany: State University of New York Press, 1996]).

[11] Charles Taylor, *Sources of the Self: The Making of Modern Identity* (Cambridge, Mass.: Har-vard University Press, 1989), 51-52.

She writes,

> Every one of us inhabits a humanly fabricated world . . . and can tell the story of what happens to him or her as he or she lives. Aware, then, on some level of the integrity and the coherence of what may seem to us to be a totally alien world in the person of another, we are called upon to use our imaginations to enter into that world, to discover how it looks and feels from the vantage point of the person whose world it is. That does not mean we approve it or even necessarily appreciate it. It does mean that we extend our experience sufficiently to grasp it as a human possibility.[12]

As the readers open themselves to the world in the text, they are able temporarily to see and explore the world of another's experience. Greene continues,

> And now and then, when I am in the presence of a work from the border, let us say, from a place outside the reach of my experience until I came in contact with the work, I am plunged into all kinds of reconceiving and revisualizing. I find myself moving from discovery to discovery; I find myself revising, and now and then renewing, the terms of my life.[13]

The reader not only enters into the world of the text but also experiences himself in that world, expanding his experience, sensibilities, sense of possibilities.

Gavin Flood notes the narrative nature of the discipline of the study of religions, explaining that

> [t]he study of religion, like history, is inherently narrative in nature. . . . The narrative—the monograph or paper—is the product of a dialogical process or interaction between the historically situated observer or scholar and the people, texts, and practices of the . . . tradition [studied].[14]

Learning religion by means of narrative texts has the advantage of specifying the particular location of a religious statement or understanding. The narrative presented by the text is encountered in the act of interpretation by the narratives that have shaped the reader's life, and thus the two "readings" of the world are brought into conversation.

When learners are exposed to several different religious texts, they are introduced to multiple perspectives on a religion, leading to broader understanding. Each of these authors represents an actual voice of the tradition, and each presents a distinctive articulation of the tradition's language, symbols, issues, and practices.

---

[12] Maxine Greene, *Releasing the Imagination: Essays on Education, the Arts, and Social Change* (San Francisco: Jossey-Bass, 1995), 4.

[13] Ibid., 4-5.

[14] Gavin Flood, *Beyond Phenomenology: Rethinking the Study of Religion* (London: Cassell, 1999), 138 (bracketed material inserted).

Readers are able to enter into texts and into the world of others through the faculty of the imagination. Maxine Green writes that "imagination is what, above all, makes empathy possible. It is what enables us to cross the empty spaces between ourselves and those we teachers have called 'other' over the years." As noted in chapter 4, Greene nuances her definition to recognize that one can never put oneself in the place of another, or understand the other world fully. She continues, "If those others are willing to give us clues, we can look in some manner through the strangers' eyes and hear through their ears."[15] We need clues from the other, and even then we can only understand "in some manner." To avoid projecting our own views onto the other we need to pursue understanding, as Clifford Geertz reminds us, "by searching out and analyzing the symbolic forms—words, images, institutions, behaviors—in terms of which, in each place, people actually represented themselves to themselves and to one another."[16] In other words, one needs to listen to the distinctive language and observe the distinctive behaviors and symbols through which people interpret themselves, much as the reader does in entering deeply into the text of another religion.

The important limits on empathy, however, raise the issue of what exactly we can experience of the religious world of another. We cannot enter into the mind, the soul, or the inner consciousness of another person. Students of religion are limited to "intersubjective" aspects of religion: those that can be communicated from one person to another, such as narratives or ritual structures.[17] Imagination and religious texts can help us to understand the experience and language of others, but they do not give us access to their inner experience.

Nevertheless, Wilfred Cantwell Smith insists that we must not be satisfied with the understanding of "data," whether of doctrines, practices, art, history, or languages. What the student of religion seeks is understanding of "what the universe means to [people], in the light of that tradition." Smith writes

> One learns to induce in oneself, by way of knowledge supplemented with appreciation—disciplined and precise knowledge supplemented with disciplined and precise, sympathetic, insight and carefully controlled imaginative perception, rigorously verified—to induce in oneself [as far as is possible] an understanding of the world as seen through Buddhist eyes, felt through Buddhist sensibilities.[18]

In sum, the first thread of learning another religion involves entering the world of that religion, encountering its difference through experience of a new context, through encounter with an adherent, through texts or other symbolic expressions of the religion that communicate a distinctive voice, and through imagination, which allows learners to enter into the world of a narrative or of a practice to

---

[15] Greene, *Releasing the Imagination*, 3.
[16] Geertz, *Local Knowledge*, 58.
[17] Flood, *Beyond Phenomenology*, 107-8.
[18] W. C. Smith, *Towards a World Theology*, 47 (bracketed material inserted).

learn its language and attempt to see—albeit partially and imperfectly—from another perspective. Entering another world exposes learners to new religious language, patterns of practice, and configurations of meaning. The entering is always partial, since the learner cannot literally put himself in the place of the other, but it is informed by an immersion in the language, practices, and ways of life of that tradition, which challenges and/or stretches the prior experience of the learner, inviting him temporarily to set aside old language and distinctions and to "try on" a new way of seeing and being.

The ultimate purpose of these various means of encountering difference and entering another world is understanding: to understand another religion as accurately as possible and as far as possible in terms of its distinctive language, symbols, and patterns of making meaning.

2. INITIAL RESPONSE FROM ONE'S OWN LOCATION

The first thread of learning explored how the encounter with difference and the act of entering another religious world challenge and stretch the learner to produce a sense of unease or discomfort. She is challenged to set aside established distinctions and categories for a time, to learn a new language and a new configuration of assumptions. She is asked to consider what and how the world means from the standpoint of another faith tradition. This newness and strangeness create a certain tension that must be addressed in the learning process.

I noted above that the two major poles of a Christian learning another religion are (1) understanding the other religion faithfully and (2) reappropriating Christian tradition in light of new understandings and relationships. The initial thread of the learning process addressed the first pole; the next thread acknowledges the second pole. Simply put, for Christians, theological learning begins from and ends with Christian identity, although that identity may be challenged, enriched, and refined between the beginning and the end of the learning process. The foundation of a Christian identity is the religious location from which the learners journey forth. The initial Christian identity of the learners may be more or less profound, more or less informed, more or less mature, but if they are Christian theological learners there is some sense in which they claim a Christian position as a starting place. That means, among other things, that Christian language, practices, symbols, and categories are their default mode of experiencing and thinking about religion.[19]

The goal of Christian theological learning is Christian identity, in the sense that theological learning intends to deepen the learner's sense of Christian tradition and how to embody that tradition in the present realities. Among those realities, and particularly relevant for the focus of this book, is the relationship of

---

[19] What I am describing here is an aspect of all religious learning, not something distinctive to Christians. Thus, adherents of all traditions experience a similar process in regard to their religious locations. I thank Denis Thalson for helping me to clarify this point (personal communication, May 28, 2002).

Christians to adherents of other religions. Only when such issues have been addressed can the learner adequately assess the validity of Christian witness, or develop the *habitus*, wisdom, and formation of Christian personality that are the goals of theological learning. For the theological learner, the accurate understanding of another religion is never the end of the process; the learner must also consider the impact of such knowledge on Christian thinking and living.

This book has argued that the task of learning is one of understanding rather than merely of acquiring information. Understanding requires solid information, but is more than simply a list of facts. Philosophers have closely examined the task of understanding under the rubric of hermeneutics (a theory of interpretation or understanding). Interpretation theorists acknowledge that understanding is inevitably shaped and limited by the prejudgments or expectations the reader brings to a text or object of interpretation. The prejudgments or expectations are shaped by the reader's "form of life," which in turn shapes the questions he thinks to ask of the text. As Gavin Flood puts it, "Understanding, as it were, is the skill of relating meanings found in a text to one's own situation and to the questions brought to bear upon it."[20] Constrained by the reader's prejudgments, "meaning is initially projected into the text and these projections are subsequently modified with further reading in light of the text."[21] "Text" here may be understood either literally or figuratively; in other words, cultural practices such as rituals or behaviors may be interpreted as texts.

Extending hermeneutical theory more explicitly to the task of learning another religion, Flood comments, "In investigating religious traditions and individual intentions and aspirations, the outside inquirer inevitably draws from and relates to the resources of her own cultural [and religious] inheritance."[22] Her understanding of religion, the language and categories she uses to think about religions, the questions she is prompted to ask about religions are all shaped by her Christianity identity.

Although it will be necessary for the learner to engage the distinctive language and understandings of the other religion, it would be a mistake to squelch those early Christian-based questions. They are, after all, expressions of interest based on the learners' experiences. In my own teaching, I have found it useful to introduce a general set of themes or issues raised by another religion and then to determine through these initial questions the starting points of the learners. On what issues and along what avenues is learning about another religion likely to be of most interest, and hence most effective?

Kenneth Bruffee would argue that learners must start from the language they know in order to find a way into the language they will need to understand another community. He writes, "They find, invent, or borrow transitional terms with which to mediate differences at the boundaries among the several nested

---

[20] Flood, *Beyond Phenomenology*, 83.

[21] Ibid., 82. Flood here invokes H.-G. Gadamer, who is in turn following Friedrich Schleiermacher and Wilhelm Dilthey.

[22] Ibid., 194 (bracketed material inserted).

groups they are members of."[23] Christians learning other religions find language from within their own tradition that will allow them to enter into conversation with the language of the other religion: this bridge or mediating language, while inadequate to the deepest levels of understanding, facilitates the process of understanding across boundaries of significant difference.

Bruffee also notes that learners "do not so much abandon the knowledge communities [or religious communities] they were raised in as learn how to negotiate new relationships with those familiar old communities they were raised in, while at the same time negotiating their way into the new communities."[24] Theological learners may fear that learning another religion will undermine their Christian identity. It will certainly challenge a static or rigid notion of that identity. Such learning, however, may enable them to establish relationships with members of other religious communities and to develop mutually edifying conversations that enrich and refine their Christian identities. They may begin to understand themselves as members of a Christian community in relationship to other religious communities.[25]

3. THREADS OF CONVERSATION AND DIALOGUE

The dual aims of Christians learning another religion (to understand the other religion well and accurately and to reappropriate Christian tradition in light of their learning) establish an inherently dialogical structure in the learning process. Critical attention and thought move between the poles of understanding the self and understanding the other. This dialogical or conversational structure also reflects the shape and dynamic of the hermeneutical process in which the learner's attempts to understand from her own location are repeatedly corrected by the voices of the other religion. This in turn nuances and broadens the learner's sense of her location, and so on: while learner and other never merge, the horizons move closer together in a dialogical/conversational movement. Such is the case, at least, when things go well. Dialogue may also end in misunderstanding; sometimes the gap of difference cannot be bridged.[26]

Because of the two poles of theological learning, there are at least two dimensions of conversation or dialogue at work in the learning process: (a) one between the Christian learners and the voices of the other religion, and (b) one among the Christian learners who are reappropriating Christian tradition and developing Christian skills and language for the new relationships they are forming. Each of

---

[23] Kenneth A. Bruffee, *Collaborative Learning: Higher Education, Interdependence, and the Authority of Knowledge,* 2nd ed. (Baltimore: Johns Hopkins University Press, 1999), 47

[24] Ibid. (bracketed material inserted to connect the citation to discussion of theological learning of other religions).

[25] Because the fears of identity loss can be intense, teachers must lay a careful foundation to help Christians understand the nature of the learning experience and how to sustain theological reflection on its implications for their lives as Christians.

[26] Matthew Farris has reminded me of this point (personal communication, June 1, 2002).

these two dimensions of conversation has a number of layers and nuances, and this section will begin to unravel some of the many threads of conversation in the learning process.

Let us begin where the last section ended. Flood notes that "the utterance of the dialogic partner must be interpreted from my perspective, it must be a response from a location."[27] That is to say, Christian learners will enter the conversation initially with distinctive Christian responses to what they have encountered in the other religion. If, however, the encounter were to end at that moment, there would be no conversation and no genuine understanding of another religion. The unfortunate result would be to reinforce uninformed Christian stereotypes of another religion. In order to avoid this outcome, the voices of the other religion must "talk back" to the learner's initial reaction to strangeness; the other religion does not remain an inert "object" to be understood through the lens of the outsider, but becomes a "subject" with voices to correct and resist misinterpretations. Flood notes, "In the study of religions, the religious other or stranger impinges herself upon me and confirms or, more likely, disrupts my preunderstanding of the religion she expresses."[28] The learner in turn responds, and a conversation ensues. This conversation may be difficult and contentious, particularly if the parties begin with considerable misunderstandings of the others' positions. Coming to understanding requires patience and persistence from all partners to the conversation.[29]

Both parties to such conversations must be mutually respectful and attentive to the voice of the other, always wary of superficial or easy agreement. They have to be willing to listen and to learn and understand the distinctive language in which the dialogue partner expresses herself. Such listening may enable the conversation to move forward, but sometimes the differences are so great that conversation will be blocked.

One colleague invited a Muslim to speak about Islam to an interfaith audience in a small Iowa community. The audience pressed the speaker on why Islamic law mandates amputating a hand as a punishment for theft. The speaker answered "Why worry about people like that?" The Iowa audience was put off by his answer and they pulled back from the conversation. Clashing cultural sensitivities—not the mere fact of amputation as a punishment in Islamic law, but what is at stake in discussing such an issue in an interreligious forum—curtailed the conversation.[30]

A conversation or dialogue in a learning process is mutually respectful, but it is also a critical conversation. Flood writes, "This kind of dialogue is critical in so far as different narratives and accounts [different religious renderings of the world] are placed under critical scrutiny; indeed each is subjected to the critical scrutiny of the other."[31] The partners in the dialogue critique each other's state-

---

[27] Flood, *Beyond Phenomenology*, 156.

[28] Ibid., 202.

[29] Choan-Seng Song has articulated seven stages of layers of dialogue in *Tell Us Our Names: Story Theology from an Asian Perspective* (Maryknoll, N.Y.: Orbis Books, 1984), 121-41.

[30] The Reverend Kathryn C. Campell, personal communication, May 20, 2002.

[31] Flood, *Beyond Phenomenology*, 149 (bracketed material inserted).

ments; they attend to each other carefully, but they also offer critical responses from their respective locations. Both also seek to understand the cultural settings that have shaped their respective views. This broader understanding of the context behind the text will help to correct misperceptions and will deepen their growing mutual understanding.

While the dialogical model implicitly assumes two persons in face-to-face conversation, it can also describe a serious engagement with the "texts" of another community. Following the hermeneutical process, scholars argue, has a fundamentally dialogical structure, and the text "speaks" and "corrects" prejudgments in much the same way as a person in conversation does. As a teacher, I have often found that close attention to a text of another tradition can be a highly effective form of dialogue. As the class first encounters the text and its difference, learners initially raise questions from their point of view. However, close engagement with the text, particularly with those passages which contain the language most distinctive to the tradition, draws students more deeply into the views of the religion. Such work can be done well in small groups, asking students to "puzzle through" difficult passages, using all commentaries available. At that point the students are ready to engage in critical conversation with the text, to critique what the text says (or seems to say), or to have the text challenge or stretch their received views. In one of the best courses of my undergraduate years, a teacher assigned half of the class the first task (critiquing the text of the basis of "our" views), and the other half the task of having the text we studied critique our views. This exercise produced a most helpful conversation.

Because that dialogue is structured by the encounter of very different perspectives shaped by distinct life experiences, the act of conversation or dialogically interpreting a text is affected by and affects both partners of the dialogue. Such dialogue or conversation, as we have seen, entails the ability of the learner to offer critiques from his own perspective and to evaluate the impact on his life of what he is learning. This brings us back to the pole of the reappropriation of Christian tradition in light of broader horizons of relationship and knowledge.

Theological learners (and arguably all Christians) are in a constant process of appropriating the Christian tradition and reappropriating it in light of present circumstances. These learners do not come to the study of other religions as theological experts with all the knowledge and answers about how to engage as Christians in dialogue. Simply put, they are refining their learning on two fronts simultaneously: learning another religion and how to engage in conversation with it, and deepening their theological reflection and their sense of Christian identity. Given the latter dimension, it would be well to tease out those threads of the conversation which are specifically theological, examining the second conversational process occurring among Christians learning another religion.

In the process of learning another religion, the theological learner starts out from and constantly circles back to her stance or location as a Christian, asking herself how her own location shapes her understanding of the other tradition but, equally important, how her understanding of the other tradition shapes her as a Christian. The learner's location shapes her understanding of the other tradition in two ways: sometimes it is a constraint or barrier to understanding, an overly constricted view that may need to be stretched in order for genuine listening and understanding to occur, and sometimes it shapes the authentic and critical voices that the learner brings to the conversation, raising questions for the other. The first restrictive constraint is a barrier to openness and to learning, but the second is an enabler of the conversation through which more profound mutual understanding can occur. The second is also the source of critical judgments from the standpoint of further Christian reflection.

The growing understanding of the other tradition can shape the theological understanding of Christian learners. As we saw in earlier chapters, James Michael Lee argues that one of the important benefits of engaging religious pluralism is to help Christians to correct and transform Christianity in the light of present circumstances so that it can move into its future promise.[32] William Pinar points out that engagement with other religions and cultures helps raise the issue, "What do I make of what I have been made?" If in the conversation one discovers something wanting or unjust in one's own community, Pinar notes, "[o]ne must then work against this particular legacy, perhaps through logic, perhaps through prayer and other religious means, perhaps through study."[33] Lee and Pinar suggest that engaging another religion makes the learner more aware of both the broader context and of his own tradition. The given and the taken for granted are now seen in a fresh light and reexamined in light of Christian values.

The task of developing skills in theological reflection to reappropriate Christian tradition is challenging in and of itself. When Christians learn other religions, attention must be paid to the development of theological reflection, both in order to represent Christian responses more effectively in the conversation and to deepen reflection on Christian beliefs and practice in relation to larger communities. Theological learners need to be in conversation not only with the other religion but also with each other; they need to hone their theological reflection while they are coming to understand another religion. They are developing new fluency, to use Bruffee's term, in two languages:[34] the language of understanding another religion (developed dialogically in conversation) and the language of reappropriating Christian tradition and developing theological understanding.

Moreover, because of the two distinct goals of Christians learning another religion, the two languages have rather different dynamics. The language of Christian tradition, and hence the traditional language of theological reflection, functions as what Richard Rorty termed "normal discourse": "that which is conducted within an agreed-upon set of conventions about what counts as a relevant contribution, what counts as answering a question, and what counts as having a

---

[32] James Michael Lee, "The Blessings of Religious Pluralism," in *Religious Pluralism and Religious Education,* ed. Norma H. Thompson (Birmingham, Ala.: Religious Education Press, 1988), 61-62.

[33] William F. Pinar, *Autobiography, Politics, and Sexuality: Essays in Curriculum Theory, 1972-1992* (New York: Peter Lang, 1994), 204.

[34] Bruffee, *Collaborative Learning,* 76.

good argument for that answer or a good criticism of it."[35] In other words, normal discourse follows well-established conventions and uses language in ways long accepted within the community.

Conversation with another religion gives rise to what Rorty calls "abnormal discourse" (Bruffee prefers "standard" and "nonstandard" to normal and abnormal): "Abnormal discourse is what happens when someone joins in the discourse who is ignorant of those conventions or who sets them aside."[36] Encountering abnormal or nonstandard discourse, Bruffee argues, requires new and more flexible language, achieved through transitional or experimental languages as the various parties seek to move from their conventional ways of speaking into the new linguistic fluency demanded by a broader conversation.[37] In the learning process described in this chapter, participants are learning the language of interreligious conversation and are also refining and giving flexibility to the "standard discourse" of their Christian community.

While conversation entails close mutual listening and attention, learning each other's languages, mutual critique, reexamining one's own positions, and developing the languages both for conversation and for Christian reflection, the major results of this learning conversation are new relationships based on mutual understanding.

4. DEVELOPING RELATIONSHIPS/LIVING OUT
ONE'S NEW UNDERSTANDING

Theological learning, as we have seen, is not only the appropriation of Christian tradition but its reappropriation in light of present circumstances. The learner continues to develop theological understanding, wisdom, and aptitudes that affect her practice of the Christian life, both within the church and in relation to the broader world. Theological learning is never simply about ideas; it is also about living one's faith.

Christians learning other religions seek more than ideas; they are also seeking to understand and develop appropriate relationships with adherents of other religions, both individually and collectively. The relational aspect of theological learning tends to argue for face-to-face experiences: meeting the religious other in the classroom, in the religious community, or in some other mutual venue. Yet all study of the other—of texts, of religious history, or of practice—has as its dual aims establishing the basis for appropriate relationships with religious others and deepening the learners' sense of Christian community and life.

For Christians, learning other religions is not a finite task that can be put behind one (been there, done that!), but is part of the formation of Christian character and preparation for Christian life. The pastor will likely need to counsel

---

[35] Richard Rorty, *Philosophy and the Mirror of Nature* (Princeton: Princeton University Press, 1979), 320. Discussed in Bruffee, *Collaborative Learning,* 143.

[36] Ibid.

[37] Bruffee, *Collaborative Learning,* 76.

interfaith marriages, to assist Christians whose sisters or sons are practicing
another religion, to counsel the teenage communicant who is drawn to Buddhism
or Taichi. The layperson is likely to have a son who is dating a Hindu, or may
need to communicate with an Islamic doctor or collaborate with a Buddhist
coworker. Learning another religion should address some of these issues for
interreligious living.

Learning other religions can also equip a person, lay or ordained, for some
leadership in his own community. He might encourage the church to get involved
in local interfaith initiatives for youth, for education, or for the environment. He
might encourage members of the parish to understand and share any ancestral
religions that have shaped their lives. He might help organize reading groups, or
groups to attend local Buddhist or Hindu festivals.

Clifford Geertz has noted that coming to understand other cultures (and other
religions) has the implication of placing us and our specific community alongside all other human communities and possibilities, "seeing ourselves amongst
others, as a local example of the forms human life has locally taken, a case
among cases, a world among worlds."[38] This also challenges us as Christians to
see ourselves as one religious community among a range of others.

To reiterate an earlier point, this idea can be challenging to many Christians.
But to see ourselves as a religious community among others is not to cede that
Christianity is the authoritative community for us as Christians; the many forms
of Christianity constitute our communities of meaning. It can simply mean recognizing that other persons and groups also have religious communities that are
meaningful and authoritative for them. It recognizes the rich and long history of
other religions, and what they have meant to their respective communities.

The practitioners of theological learning discussed in chapter 4 provide some
sense of the nature of the new relationships and practices that emerge from learning another religion. Grant Shockley notes that engagement with religious and
cultural diversity "seeks an ampler and more functional understanding of the
nature and meaning of religion or theology in its situation of diversity—cultural,
ethnic, racial, linguistic; seeks ways of enabling persons to live together more
creatively in and with diversity."[39] For Shockley the understanding of the other is
directed toward new and better ways of persons living together. James Michael
Lee suggests that engaging religious pluralism is fundamentally about establishing loving relationships: "If we are to teach learners to engage in religiously pluralistic activities, we should teach them how to love other religious traditions and
their adherents rather than simply to know them."[40] It is, of course, a basic Christian principle to love neighbors, but it is striking to see a call for Christians to
love other religions and their adherents.

The idealism of Shockley's and Lee's visions points to making the world a

---

[38] Geertz, *Local Knowledge*, 16.

[39] Grant S. Shockley, "Religious Pluralism and Religious Education: A Black Protestant Perspective," in *Religious Pluralism and Religious Education*, ed. Thompson, 146.

[40] Lee, "Blessings," 71.

better place: living together more effectively and coming to love one another. However, as is all too evident, the world is a long way from such ideals. Thus, living out relationships with members of other religions is no easier than coming to understand them. A long and complex history of misunderstandings and tensions often gives rise to pain and confusion and requires enormous patience, understanding, and good will on the part of all parties.[41] We may be fortunate to establish positive relationships with an individual family member, neighbor, or coworker; but even these relationships may be troubled by the complex historical and contemporary tensions between religious communities. The personal and the political can never be fully disentangled. As we develop particular relationships with members of other religions, we should not ignore the larger structural and historical issues that demand attention and resolution. Such large issues are always beyond the scope of an individual or small group, but they are part of the context within which we establish and live out our relationships.

As a freshman in college I took a course in Protestantism, Catholicism, and Judaism in the United States. A question on the final exam stated the major provisions of civil rights legislation pending in Congress and asked, "Based on what you have learned, what *should be* the positions of these religious groups on this legislation?" Although challenging, the question brought the learning down to issues shaping lives in that contemporary context. We too often teach and learn other religions as though they had no impact on our actual lives. Attending to life issues such as marriage and family, gender roles, ideas about life and death, and ideals of human excellence, can help us to better understand both ourselves and our religious neighbors.

The developing of new relationships and new patterns of behavior can be effectively explored through experiential learning—field education, well-designed site visits, or community learning. An experiential learning course on the diverse religious communities in Chicago used site visits and community service to develop understanding of other communities. The relationships developed in students' research and community service were so meaningful to the students that many continued to volunteer in other religious communities after the end of the course.[42]

The learning process provides the basis for new relationships and for transformative actions and the understanding and linguistic flexibility to work with others who bring very different life practices and views to any common cause.

5. INTERNALIZING THE PROCESS

This chapter has attempted to unravel some of the threads of the process of Christians learning another religion, with the purpose of focusing attention on the various aspects of that learning process. The final thread of the process is one that

---

[41] I thank my colleague Fumitaka Matsuoka for reminding me to underscore this point (personal communication, June 15, 2002).

[42] Jeffrey Carlson, "From Site Unseen to Experiential Learning: Religious Studies in the 'Discover Chicago' Model," *Teaching Theology and Religion* 1, no. 2 (June 1998): 120-27.

weaves the other threads together so that, so to speak, what has been learned does not unravel, but forms a thread of ongoing learning, wisdom, and practice. Another way to put it is that in this process learners not only encounter difference, respond from their locations, enter into and develop the many levels of conversation and theological reflection, and enter into new relationships and transformative actions, but also *learn the process*. This is essential because learners can never learn everything there is to know about another religion, nor can they learn all the religions there are to know. Given the diversity of contemporary life, a Christian will continue to encounter new representatives of religions and new religions. No workshop, course, or advanced degree can provide enough learning, but one can learn how to learn.

We not only learn *through* conversation, but we learn *how to converse*.[43] Learners of other religions are encouraged to develop their skill and fluency in a new sort of conversation.[44] Richard Rorty notes that fluency in conversation gives learners confidence that they know how to negotiate the next situation; they know how to handle themselves in similar situations. By extension, it is not what the learner has come to know about Hinduism, Buddhism, or any other religion but her skill in engaging dialogically the texts, practices, and adherents of other religions that provide her with a sense of how to proceed when she engages yet another religion.

The necessity and nature of this internalization of the learning process can also be articulated in terms of the wisdom-based theories of theological learning—theological learning as *paideia*, or the formation of *habitus*. Learning wisdom is a matter not of learning information, facts about something or other, but of forming dispositions, attitudes, and character that enable one both to understand and to live in the world.

Finally, internalization of the process is important because, building on Maxine Greene and bell hooks, the aim of the learning process articulated in this chapter is to give learners voice and the ability to listen, to establish networks of relationships, to build bridges, and to live and move effectively in the world, making it a better place. It is not a process for absorbing information but an empowerment of learners to engage broader and broader spheres of knowledge and experience and, in turn, refine their relationships to these spheres.

This chapter unraveled various threads or aspects of that process so that each could be examined carefully in its own right. Most approaches to learning other religions focus almost entirely on one of these threads, obscuring other dimensions of the learning process. While perfect balance is a utopian ideal, the unraveling of the threads of the process helps evaluate the effectiveness of various learning approaches, whether in the classroom or beyond. Without such awareness, it will not be possible to improve or refine the ways in which Christians learn other religions.

---

[43] Bruffee, *Collaborative Learning,* 133.
[44] Ibid., 76.

6

Classroom Learning

Improving Traditional Approaches

Previous chapters have explored teaching and learning theory, theories of the study of comparative religions, and issues in theological learning as a backdrop for articulating the threads of the process of Christians learning other religions. The last section of this book deals with the practical issues of actual learning situations, with this chapter focusing on classroom and school-sponsored learning.

A growing number of theological and divinity schools understand the facts of religious diversity and embrace in principle the desirability of pastors, lay leaders, and educated Christians understanding Christianity in relation to other religions. Yet it is not at all clear how to do this well. The core curriculum of theological education, as we saw in chapter 4, is the subject of considerable debate, in large part because theological education is under pressure to include multiple concerns, issues, and perspectives—women's issues, multiculturalism, globalization, the environment, social justice, social analysis, congregational dynamics, contextual theologies, alternative ministries, death and dying, health and science—the list is almost endless. Learning other religions often is simply added to this long list of concerns. Addressing any or all issues on this list is often impeded by the fact that the fourfold Protestant division of theological learning (Bible, history, theology, pastoral skills) or the fivefold Roman Catholic division (Bible, historical theology, systematic theology, moral theology, pastoral theology) still dominates most theological curricula, pushing other concerns into the shrinking number of electives available to M.Div. students. Some students create time to address particular issues by adding an academic master of arts or master of theological studies degree to their theological educations, but such degrees are usually pursued out of a personal interest rather than as a well-considered supplement to a sound theological education. Despite many experiments in curricular reform, theological schools are still struggling to articulate a new curricular structure that addresses contemporary demands.

Given this situation, theological faculties generally are not doing well at providing opportunities for students to learn other religions. On the one hand, a number of core courses have incorporated some religious diversity, but usually not in ways that faculty or students find wholly satisfying. On the other hand, separate elective courses are difficult to design for the needs of theological students. Most of the traditional models for such courses are under fire for good reasons; we will explore how the learning threads articulated in the last chapter help identify the problems with traditional course models.

Faculty members who are academically trained in the study of other religions and in their languages and cultures are relatively rare in theological schools. But even such faculty—myself included—are dissatisfied with our attempts at helping Christians learn other religions. Most of us were trained in programs that followed a rigid and outmoded model that the study of other religions must be "objective" and "scientific" and not tainted by theological dimensions. Although many hold that this method is no longer defensible, faculty continue to struggle and sometimes overcompensate to avoid the excesses and errors of the historical European condescension toward the other religions that was fueled by unexamined religious and cultural assumptions. The 150-year history discussed by Eric Sharpe is replete with tensions and debates that continue to affect attitudes and practices, even though many of the issues have disappeared or have been significantly transformed.[1]

It is extremely difficult to conceive of teaching in a dramatically new way. For many reasons (good and bad) teaching practices evolve slowly. Old habits die hard, and institutional pressures (internal and external) reinforce a conservative and gradual approach to educational reform. Faculty who seek to address other religions effectively in Christian theological education are searching; we know many of the issues, yet we do not yet have the answers. This chapter examines issues about classroom learning on two different levels. First, the threads of the learning process and the various learning theories behind them will be used to evaluate and critique some common approaches and resources used for teaching other religions in theological education, both in core courses and in electives. The evaluation and critique will suggest principles for improving or refining these approaches. Second, the chapter offers several radically different approaches. Many faculties or schools will be unable to institute such ideas immediately, but it is hoped that these proposals will stimulate fresh thinking, planting the seeds of future developments in theological teaching and learning. The chapter concludes with a "middle way," some concrete steps that may help theological faculties and schools move in the direction of helping Christians learn other religions.

REASSESSING THE WAYS OTHER RELIGIONS HAVE BEEN TAUGHT

This section builds on the previous discussions of learning theory and the threads of the learning process to evaluate and critique some of the most com-

---

[1] Eric J. Sharpe, *Comparative Religion: A History,* 2nd ed. (Chicago: Open Court Publishing, 1986). Discussed in chapter 3.

mon approaches to teaching other religions in theological settings, offering some guidelines for improvement. The critiques rest on the principles discussed in previous chapters: (1) to engage a diversity of actual voices of the religions (adherents, texts, or practices); (2) to engage religions as living religions, in the actual lives of people in particular contexts; (3) to address the Christian starting point of Christian learners; (4) to develop understanding through various levels of mutually critical conversations in which the views and perspectives of Christianity and the other religions engage one another; (5) to engage Christian learners in theological reflection about the implications of what they have learned for Christian life and practice; and (6) to give learners a sense of the process so that they can continue learning in other contexts.

REVISITING COMMON APPROACHES
TO TEACHING OTHER RELIGIONS

1. The Survey Course

Theological students convinced of the importance of religious diversity often ask for a survey of world religions. The reasons are fairly easy to understand. The survey course is an efficient and relatively painless way to "know something about" other religions, packing it all into a single elective. For undergraduates, survey courses provided information in a concise and helpful framework that was relatively easy to comprehend and not so demanding as to distract from their major, which they considered the "meat" of their education. Survey courses also lessen the pressure on teachers of core courses to address other religions.

However, survey courses almost always fail to meet the principles and goals described in this book—and fail on multiple counts. "Knowing about" other religions assumes that what learners need is *information about* a religion—a few key facts and figures, texts, dates, and concepts. However, this model of education (transmission of information) is not adequate to the goals of understanding and interpretation stressed by all the theorists discussed in this volume. Students leave surveys with some facts, but not with *understanding* of the other tradition or of its internal complexities. In treating many religions or all the "significant" world religions, surveys tend to oversimplify traditions, and ignore the many voices and lived experiences of the cumulative aspects of tradition. Diana Eck provides an example of the shortcomings of this approach.

> The five pillars make it easy to remember the fundamentals of Islam. . . . They must not make our task of understanding Islam too simple, however, for there are many Muslims for whom this structure of life is not the definitive formula for Islamic life. They might not pray five times a day or ever go to the mosque. They might visit shrines of Muslim saints for blessing and inspiration, or they might learn their grounding in Islam from the women's cultures of their grandmothers and aunts, women who have listened to Qurʾanic recitation in their homes, who have taken seriously the

notion that there is no priesthood in Islam, who know in their hearts that there are no intermediaries between human beings and God, and whose lives of faith are not at all set by the dictates of Islamic legal tradition.[2]

Traditions are summarized and essentialized by their interpreters—the instructor or the textbook editor, or both. This sort of simplification repeats serious historical errors in the study of religions and does little to promote understanding. Additionally, and particularly in theological schools, the survey tends to exclude Christianity, perpetuating the notion that learning religions is about "them," not "us." This perpetuates a privileged role for Christianity, which is not only studied in much greater detail but is carefully removed from the "other" category of "world religions."[3] The sense of privilege may be unconscious, but it was verified for me when, as dean of the Graduate Theological Union, I responded to the complaints of faculty about the lack of basic grounding in the Christian heritage on the part of many seminary students. I suggested a survey of Christianity to provide a basic overview. My colleagues were horrified by the suggestion that Christianity could be taught in one semester; yet several hoped for a one-semester survey of the world's religions. Theological educators and learners need to be clear about the implications of assumptions that other religions can be studied in ways they would consider utterly unsuitable for the study of their own tradition.

In part because of their broad sweep, and in part because the expectation that the survey not be too demanding or distracting, surveys seldom have the space to engage difference authentically. Such courses lack sufficient time for engagement with the voices of the tradition in the forms of guest lecturers, primary texts, or film. The survey tends to erase or elide differences by organizing the course around themes, issues, or strands that create a sense of cohesion or continuity in the course. The simplifications create a framework of understanding that reassures learners, but they do so at the expense of understanding across lines of difference.

Finally, surveys offer insufficient space and attention to the dialogical or conversational dimensions of learning, both between the learners and the other traditions, and among the learners about the implications of the new knowledge for their understanding of their Christian identities. In short, broad surveys tend to distance the religions much like the color-coded maps of my youth: they box the religions into handy compartments or containers so that they can be grasped quickly without causing the sort of discomfort or challenge that can lead to genuine understanding.[4]

Faculty who teach broad surveys have struggled with these questions and have

---

[2] Diana L. Eck, *A New Religious America: How A "Christian Country" Has Become the World's Most Religiously Diverse Nation* (San Francisco: HarperSanFranciso, 2001), 280.

[3] For a discussion of this issue, see Gavin Flood, *Beyond Phenomenology: Rethinking the Study of Religion* (London: Cassell, 1999), 233ff.

[4] Clifford Geertz, *Local Knowledge: Further Essays in Interpretive Anthropology*, 2nd ed. (New York: Basic Books, 2000), 45.

tried to develop more responsible ways for offering such courses. While there is no consensus about the "solution" to these problems, the following suggestions are based on the principles and issues discussed in this book and on the cumulative wisdom of struggling faculty.

First, it is best to limit the broad sweep of a survey to allow more time and space for effective learning. In my experience, no more than two or three traditions should be covered in a semester. That means some hard choices, but if learners are to understand different religions and develop a sense of how to continue and deepen their learning, studying two or three religions may be far preferable to getting some prepackaged information about six or seven. If a school feels strongly that all major traditions should be taught, an approach might be to offer them in some rotation, varying the traditions taught year by year.

In the context of theological education, it is advisable to include in such a course the relations of other religions to Christianity. Thus "surveys" might include (a) religions of the Book: Judaism, Christianity, and Islam; (b) indigenous religions and Christianities in the Americas, the Pacific, and Africa; (c) Asians religions and Christianities.[5] Each of these topics has a broad sweep and would require considerable selectivity in planning and execution. The challenge, of course, is in identifying faculty to teach such courses. Many faculty members are either specialists in a single tradition (e.g., Islam or Buddhism) or in area studies (e.g., Indian religions or Chinese religions). Each of the surveys listed above is going to stretch a faculty person significantly beyond her expertise, both in knowledge of the traditions taught (history, texts, languages) and in knowledge of or connections with representatives of the religious communities and local resources, film, and literature. By its very nature the broad survey pulls faculty onto very thin ice, rendering them excessively dependent on textbooks and third-hand resources. The best practice is probably for a school to consider a number of surveys it would like to offer, and then identify faculty willing to invest the time and energy to develop the knowledge and connections necessary to teach such a course responsibly.

Second, many teachers and texts now discuss contemporary, living traditions, rather than offering a few facts about the origins and early teachings of religions. Textbooks increasingly discuss religions as they are understood and practiced today. For instance, Arvind Sharma's *Our Religions* presents several religions as introduced by eminent scholars from each of the traditions. Each scholar addresses the history, development, and issues within his tradition and then discusses its contemporary practice, debates, and relations with other religions.[6] Another example is the collection entitled *World Religions Today,* which explores how each of the religious traditions has addressed the challenges of modernity and postmodern trends in a postcolonial world. The history of each tradition is

---

[5] Philip Wickeri and I cotaught a course on Asian Christianities in Diverse Cultural and Religious Contexts at the GTU in the spring of 2003.

[6] Arvind Sharma, ed., *Our Religions: The Seven World Religions Introduced by Preeminent Scholars from each Tradition* (San Francisco: HarperSanFrancisco, 1993).

discussed as the context for its engagement with the issues of modernity.[7] It is now eminently feasible to teach a survey of world religions in America, utilizing texts such as *World Religions in America*, edited by Jacob Neusner.[8] The best texts include several voices and perspectives, including perspectives of women or the experiences of ordinary practitioners who may not reflect the teachings of the normative scriptures or the religious elite. Surveys of contemporary religions often make extensive use of film, literature, and site visits to underscore the access learners have to lived religious experience.

Third, the best surveys are now careful to include issues of contention, both historical and contemporary, so as not to present a single voice or angle on the tradition. Selecting the appropriate issues and debates is itself a delicate matter, for the biases of the teacher or textbook author may offer a distorted perspective. Nevertheless, including issues is at least an improvement on the "three-to-five-essential-teachings" approach common in the past. The *World Religions Today* text structures a survey around the tensions and debates of each religion in response to the challenges of modernity. Naomi Southard and Richard Payne of the GTU created an introduction to "world's religions" that addressed issues of religious pluralism in the United States in a postcolonial world, focusing on issues of representation and the relationship of each religion to the "dominant" U.S. culture.[9]

Fourth, surveys need to allow time for mutually critical engagement and conversation with the other traditions: conversation with adherents, texts, or practices. This means including well-planned exercises for critical engagement with primary texts in translation or a work of fiction, for a well-planned site visit with follow-up for analysis and reflection, for engagement with adherents of the tradition either in class or as a field assignment. Whatever forms are selected, these learning exercises and assignments must be structured to help students meet the goals of the course, including the goal of developing understanding across lines of difference.

Developing understanding, as we have seen, means facing the unease of difference (engaging the distinctive—and strange—ways in which religions represent and express themselves) and gradually correcting misperceptions through mutually critical conversation. Students often prefer a clear (prefabricated) framework of understanding, provided by either the text or the instructor, so that they have a "handle" on the material. They look to the instructor to provide that framework, that clarifying interpretation. I have learned to sidestep this expectation by structuring sessions so that classes begin with students' conversations about the meanings they found in the texts or readings. At the end of a session, I

---

[7] John L. Esposito, Darrell J. Fasching, Todd Lewis, eds., *World Religions Today* (Oxford: Oxford University Press, 2002.)

[8] Jacob Neusner, ed., *World Religions in America: An Introduction* (Louisville: Westminster John Knox Press, 1994). Articles on the various religions are written by different scholars.

[9] Naomi Southard and Richard Payne, "Teaching the Introduction to Religions: Religious Pluralism in a Post-Colonial World," *Teaching Theology and Religion* 1, no. 1 (February 1998): 51-57.

offer a very brief (ten-minute) "prelection," or preparation for reading,[10] which offers some important aspects of context, defines a few key terms that students will encounter in the readings, and raises questions and issues for interpreting the readings. The prelection helps students to engage the distinctive language of the text, but does not provide the "meaning" of the text. The engagement with meaning will occur first in the written answers to the questions, brought by students to the class, and then in the class discussion. If in discussion the students do not fully engage the central issues in the text, I gently lead them back into those issues.

Fifth, the learning experiences and assignments included in surveys in a theological setting should focus attention on how such learning relates to the student's understanding of her distinctive religious location. In religiously diverse classrooms, learners may be encouraged to help research and present their own traditions, through oral histories or other types of research. They learn their traditions more deeply through teaching them, and also learn from and with one another. In more monolithically "Christian" classrooms, students might be invited to do critical comparative reflection or journaling, discussing these in small groups so as to develop their capacity for theological reflection on the materials. Assignments should probably be of two kinds: (a) those that demonstrate the capacity to understand the religions well and the ability to use their distinctive languages and forms of expression, and (b) those that demonstrate the ability to reflect on the implications of what has been learned for Christian self-understanding, theological reflection, and practice.

Finally, there is the issue of what happens after the student completes the course. Is this simply a subject matter to which the theological curriculum or student makes a perfunctory, even if respectful, bow, or does learning other religions need to engage and enrich broader theological learning? If a theological school requires that students study other religions, how is that learning then engaged in other aspects of the theological curriculum?

2. The Introduction to Another Religion: Who Should Teach It?

Another common elective is the introduction to one religion. This course structure is somewhat less problematic than the broad survey because there is time to present the development, diversity, and range of voices and issues within the tradition; to introduce students to a variety of texts and resources; and to give them a chance to engage deeply the distinctive languages, practices, symbols, and institutions through which adherents of this religion represent and interpret themselves to each other and to the external world. It is also more possible to staff, since it is comparatively easy to find a teacher with expertise in a single tradition.

---

[10] I am indebted for the term to my colleague Jeffrey Richey, with whom I cotaught one semester.

The chief problem with this type of course in the theological curriculum is that it may address only one pole of the learning process articulated in the last chapter: to understand the other religion faithfully. Can such a course be structured (and is the instructor qualified) to nurture both dimensions of conversation described in the threads of the learning process: (a) conversations between learners and the voices/texts of the other religion and (b) conversations among learners about the theological implications of their growing understanding for their reconstruction of Christian identities and development of more flexible language within the Christian community? In my experience, most courses of this type focus on the first with very little attention to the second. When that happens, theological learners face difficulties in connecting their new understanding of another religion to their theological self-understanding as Christians.

Another issue is closely related to nurturing the theological reflection of Christian learners in such a course: addressing resistances and fears involved in crossing boundaries to engage another religion. Kenneth Bruffee encourages professors "to learn how to help students tolerate the risks and stresses that everyone who tries to cross knowledge community boundaries experiences."[11] These fears and resistances are underscored when theological learners are so intent on forging a clearer sense of their Christian identity that engaging another religion can seem very threatening and intimidating. It is extremely important for the instructor to provide clarity about the goals and importance of the process and a safe place to express fears and anxieties when students move into unknown territory.

The course on another religion raises a major issue for theological schools: who is the best facilitator for such a course? This is a complex issue that requires discussion in some depth.

One challenge to teaching other religions in Christian theological schools is that very few Christian theological schools have regular faculty trained in other religions, their languages and cultures. Given this reality, most schools either call upon their own faculty to stretch far beyond their formal academic expertise (never a comfortable situation for faculty), or they resort to adjunct faculty. University-related divinity schools have some advantages in this regard, as do seminaries and schools with close relationships to a university or college with a department of religious studies. The universities and colleges have faculty who can offer regular courses. Students at such schools have access to rich resources for learning other religions. Even at schools with such resources, however, the learning of other religions is seldom integrated into theological learning. The courses are electives. Even if strongly recommended or required, courses on other religions are quite separate from theological learning, which the students naturally see as the substance of their program. While these schools have ready-made teachers for courses, the teachers have no relation to the theological curriculum.

---

[11] Kenneth A. Bruffee, *Collaborative Learning: Higher Education, Interdependence, and the Authority of Knowledge*, 2nd ed. (Baltimore: Johns Hopkins University Press, 1999), 164.

When freestanding theological schools turn to adjuncts to teach other religions, there is a dominant assumption that these courses should properly be taught by an adherent of the religion. This is understandable, as theological schools hire Christian faculty to teach the Christian tradition; these faculty are not only scholars trained in a discipline but also, like their students, persons of faith continually reflecting on and refining their sense of Christian tradition and practice.

However, the learning process articulated in this book prompts us to raise a number of questions about hiring adherents of other religions to teach their traditions to theological students. On one level, the adherent of another religion represents an authentic voice of the tradition both in her own teaching and in the overall design of the course or learning experience. The course will not fall prey to unexamined biases in which European Christians, or European converts, still deeply shaped by their cultural biases, become the interpreters, evaluators of, and spokespersons for other religions.[12] There are, however, a number of other issues to be considered.

The first issue comes from Wilfred Cantwell Smith's reminder that every adherent of a tradition has a particular and limited experience of the vast cumulative tradition of the religion she espouses.[13] When the representative of a religion is invited for a guest appearance or is visited in his religious community, the assumption is that students are encountering one specific voice of a tradition. Planning an entire course, however, requires a broader understanding of the history and sweep of the tradition, of the diverse views and voices that have shaped and continue to shape its life. This broader understanding comes with education. Schools must ask, therefore, whether the prospective adjunct professor has the broad education in the cumulative tradition that would enable him to plan a course that brings many voices of the tradition into the learning experience. Sometimes theological schools hire the local rabbi, imam, or priest to teach his tradition without regard to whether the person has a depth of understanding of the entire tradition. As teachers, they need to be more than representatives of their traditions; they must also be scholars who have the responsibility to bring an appropriate range of voices and issues into the classroom.

A second set of issues is the need for critical conversation between Christianity and the other religion in the learning process. Adherents may be relied upon to bring into conversation the distinctive language, practices, symbols, and institutions of their tradition on its own terms, but how effective will they be in explaining these terms to outsiders or in understanding and correcting the misconceptions of the Christian students? A colleague at one seminary reported the disastrous failure of a course taught by a Russian Orthodox priest (and this course within the broader Christian communion, not quite so different or alien as

---

[12] I am indebted to my colleague Richard Payne for making the point about European converts (personal communication, May 29, 2002).

[13] Wilfred Cantwell Smith, *Towards a World Theology: Faith and the Comparative History of Religion* (Philadelphia: Westminster Press, 1981; Maryknoll, N.Y.: Orbis Books, 1989), 24-25.

another religion entirely). The priest knew his tradition well and was faithful in explaining it in its own terms, so much so that students found his teaching utterly opaque and off-putting. They left the course with a dramatically increased antipathy toward Orthodox Christianity—not the outcome the seminary had hoped for! Likewise a Buddhist priest might be very gifted in teaching Buddhists to understand and practice their own tradition and very awkward or ineffective in explaining Buddhism to outsiders.

Teaching across religious lines is a particular skill and talent. There are thankfully a number of adherents of non-Christian religions in this country who excel at such teaching and interpretation, in part perhaps because of the pressures to "explain themselves" as members of a religious minority.[14] If schools wish to hire an adherent to teach, they need to recognize that they are seeking *someone who can teach across religious lines* (the most salient qualification) rather than simply someone who represents the tradition. Even if a school finds a person with that vocation, they need to ensure that the person does not set himself up as *the* authentic voice and embodiment of the tradition. He should be a door or window onto the richness of the tradition, rather than its authoritative spokesperson.

Yet there is another issue. Is the adherent of the other religion in a position to nurture and sustain both sides and both levels of conversations in the learning process? That is to say, can she help the students to enter into conversation from their particular locations as Christians? Theological students are in the midst of an intensive process of theological reflection and learning. They are aware, and becoming ever more aware, that they do not have all the theological answers. Thus, they do not enter a course on other religions fully prepared to represent Christianity or to formulate all of the questions and responses from the Christian side. Their participation in the dialogue needs to be nurtured and fostered. They are also challenged by their growing understanding of the other religion into even deeper theological reflection, revisiting the theological language and assumptions of their tradition as they seek to articulate theological language more suited for articulating Christianity in relation to its many religious neighbors. An adherent of another religion is only rarely equipped to mentor or facilitate that conversation.

Kenneth Bruffee is helpful in articulating the issues involved in terms of learning theory. He notes, "What teachers do is help students engage one another in reacculturative conversation. That is, teachers help students engage in nonstandard conversation at the boundaries between knowledge communities."[15] As readers may recall from discussions of Bruffee in chapters 2 and 5, nonstandard conversations occur when persons (of another religious community) who do not know or share the assumptions of the learner's religious community—in this case, a Christian theological school—challenge those assumptions. Thus students need to learn fluency in a new language that allows them to negotiate this broader conversation; the role of the teacher, Bruffee argues, is to help students

---

[14] Eck, *A New Religious America,* 128, 236.
[15] Bruffee, *Collaborative Learning,* 120.

gain fluency in this new language of interreligious conversation and understanding. A teacher in a course like this needs more than fluency in the language of her own religious community. As Bruffee notes, "the most important skill that [theological] professors bring to bear, and can impart to their students, is skill in linguistic improvisation: translation."[16] This is a skill quite different from merely representing and interpreting one's own religious community. Moreover, professors in such courses need skill in helping students with the stresses and strains of learning to talk across boundaries of difference; or, as Bruffee puts it, "they help students learn how to navigate the white water of nonstandard boundary discourse."[17] Finally, Bruffee acknowledges that in addition to learning to enter the broader conversations at the boundaries between communities, faculty must "help students renegotiate their relations with the communities they come from."[18] In relation to Christians learning other religions, attention must also be paid to the reflexive movement, the reappropriation of Christian tradition in light of a broader horizon.[19]

The learning process articulated in this book strongly suggests that theological schools need to consider how best to foster the theological reflection of Christians learning other religions. Do such courses require coteachers? This is perhaps the best option and would ensure that a regular faculty member takes responsibility to see that the learning goals of the course intended by the school are appropriately addressed. Should theological reflection be addressed outside of this particular class, perhaps in some planned relationship to other courses the student is taking? This would have the advantage of integrating the learning into the "core" theological curriculum and would require prior collaboration on the part of the instructors. Should schools ask advanced students with some background in this kind of learning to help foster the Christian theological discussion that grows along with the interreligious conversation? This plan would be based on collaborative learning and would give advanced students some sense of their increasing facility in nurturing theological reflection. Do schools need to devise exercises to be offered in conjunction with such courses? A school might require theological reflection papers, journals, and so on that would be reviewed by the student's advisor or put in a portfolio for annual student review.

Two other models are sometimes used. In the first, a core theological faculty member teaches a course on another religion, bringing in guest speakers and using film, site visits, and texts to introduce authentic voices of the other religion. If such a faculty member has no formal training in the religion she is teaching, it is best if she can consult carefully with persons who do have such training—

---

[16] Ibid., 148 (bracketed material inserted to replace "college and university," thus adapting the quote to the context of this discussion).

[17] Ibid., 163.

[18] Ibid., 197.

[19] Denis Thalson reminds me that international students studying in North American seminaries often engage a broader Christianity than the one they have known. When they return home, they have reentry problems; they have to learn to negotiate their Christian identities in their various home contexts (personal communication, May 28, 2002).

academic training in religious studies plus the language and culture—and with well-educated adherents of the tradition. The danger here is that the faculty member will have a tendency to fall too easily into her Christian lens for interpreting and presenting issues. Thus, she must be careful to give due consideration to the authentic voices of the other religion and to ask for help when it is needed.[20]

The second model is to hire a trained scholar of religious studies who is also a Christian. In this case, the faculty person needs to be sure that he is attending sufficiently to the theological reflection of the students. If he does not also have a theological degree, he may have to turn to theological colleagues for advice and counsel on how to incorporate and nurture such theological reflection, and perhaps invite colleagues in (at least for a time) to facilitate the conversation and model some strategies for guiding it. In addition, the scholar of religious studies needs to be clear and appropriately humble about his role. He must be attentive to bringing in many authentic voices and points of view and as much of the living tradition as possible. It would be advisable to consult with representatives of the tradition in the local community for input on the design of the course and on the live issues that might be presented. The scholar of religion is likely to have a good grasp of the texts and the sweep of history of the tradition, of its language and practices. However, it is dangerous to succumb to pressures to present summaries or surveys, to let his scholarly grasp of the religion substitute for its authentic voices and living experiences.

To put it too simply, the teacher's role is not primarily to convey information about the religion or her own hard-won understanding of the religion but to facilitate the students' coming to an understanding of the religion. Teaching others to come to understand is a particular and challenging task that is quite separate from what training in religious studies provides: skill in the language, knowledge of history and cultural practices, and coming to one's own understanding of another religion in its cultural setting. The teacher of other religions in a theological setting is not teaching students to become religious studies scholars, but is nurturing the skills of entering into critical conversation with and understanding other religions.

3. The "Add-on" within a Course

Some faculty members who teach required core courses for the M.Div. program have, to their credit, sought to include materials about other religions. Unfortunately, given the pressures of what must be covered in required core courses, the other religion is usually an add-on, a single text or session devoted

---

[20] A faculty person in this position might reflect on some of the issues by reading Deanna A. Thompson's article "Teaching What I'm Not: Embodiment, Race, and Theological Conversation in the Classroom," *Teaching Theology and Religion* 3, no. 3 (October 2000): 164-69. Although this article specifically addresses interracial issues, many of the issues are, *mutatis mutandis*, applicable to the challenges of teaching a religion other than one's own in the theological setting.

to another religion. This strategy recalls a model for addressing women's issues lamented by feminists—the "add women and stir" approach, that is, including a few materials on women without changing the structure or assumptions of the course. Such strategies demonstrate good intentions and alert students to important issues, but they do not address the educational issues presented by difference, be that gender difference or religious pluralism.

However, given the multiple pressures on core courses, the add-on is likely to remain the closest many schools can come for the moment to "mainstreaming" engagement with other religions. Add-ons in core required courses ensure that theological students will at least be introduced to issues of religious pluralism and of the relationship of Christianity to other religions; in that sense, add-ons are far preferable to electives. However, faculty who use add-ons need a good framework to evaluate how to use them well.

One common if understandable shortcoming is that faculty choose sources on other religions that are readable and accessible to their students, so that they can use them easily in the limited time allotted. The discussion of the encounter with difference in the last chapter raised the salient issue: if the readings are too accessible or a visitor presents the other religion in terms too easily grasped in Christian terms, the students never really engage difference. These students do not even begin the learning process articulated in the last chapter. Such learning experiences unintentionally continue a long-standing error of seeing other religions solely through Christian lenses. When that occurs, Christians expect interfaith understanding, dialogue, and interaction always to be on their terms. Such learning does not address the implications of religious pluralism. Choosing less accessible texts or more challenging guest lecturers, however, requires allotting more time and space for other religions in the course. This is surely a genuine challenge. But designing a more engaging learning experience can also deepen the students' critical reflection on the Christian learning in the course.

It is also difficult for faculty with no training in another religion to select appropriate readings, learning experiences, or guest lecturers. Faculty persons like myself, whether located in theological schools, or in nearby or related institutions, can help colleagues in other fields select readings, films, or lecturers that would bring the voices of the other religions into the theological classroom. Given that these texts are less accessible, they might also discuss with their colleagues how best to present these materials so as to help students make the connections between the distinctive language and viewpoints of the other religions and the Christian issues germane to the course.

Given the principles outlined above, it is also important and desirable that at least two voices of a tradition be heard and studied, so that another religion is not presented as an essentialized monolith. Religious traditions comprise many strands and voices; only in this diversity can we grasp them as living traditions.

Finally, add-ons need to be designed to include both the give-and-take (mutual clarification and correction) of conversation with the voices of the other religion and conversations about the theological implications of understanding this religion for the students as Christians. Both aspects of this conversation can support the primary learning goals of the course, although it is often the case that the faculty member sees the time spent on understanding the other religion as something of a digression from the primary course goals. Careful selection of the other religion and the voices and issues to be engaged can help to ensure that understanding religious difference will also enhance learners' abilities to think critically and reflectively about their own tradition. In fact, if chosen well, the materials on the other religion might help to articulate the theological learning the faculty intends for the course. Finding just the right religion and set of voices and issues will require a significant initial investment of faculty time, but it will pay off in the long run.

Perhaps the best model for integrating other religions into core courses is addressing these issues as they naturally arise. My colleague Chris Ocker, for instance, includes Christian responses to Muslims and Jews in the history of medieval Christianity. Several Hebrew Bible scholars address the issues of other religions in the writings of the Old Testament. Paul's attitude toward Jews, and Jesus' own Jewish practice and relationships, are natural topics in a New Testament course.[21]

4. The "Dialogue" Course

An increasingly popular course format is the "dialogue" course, cotaught by representatives of two different religions. This format has a number of advantages. The genuine voices of the two traditions are represented: in a theological school one is Christian and the other represents another tradition (e.g., Judaism, Buddhism, etc.). The pedagogical structure of the course is dialogical, or conversational; thus, the all-important dialogical elements of learning are built in. As in all cotaught courses, much depends on how well the two instructors work together. They need to develop a relationship in which they work together to promote the dialogical structure of the course and not simply defer to each other or divide the materials into "mine" and "yours." Second, they need to plan the course thoroughly as a dialogical course. What are the course goals, and are they clearly understood and owned by both instructors? How do the materials and the assignments contribute to students' meeting those goals? I have team taught rather extensively and know all too well that it is sometimes difficult to work out these issues between two instructors.

The learning process articulated in this book reminds us to ask a number of questions about any "dialogical" course. First and foremost, does the learning conversation or dialogue fully engage and include the students, or do they simply or primarily observe the coteachers engaging in dialogue? This is the most serious pedagogical trap for such courses. On the one hand, the instructors want

---

[21] I am grateful to my colleague Philip Wickeri for reminding me of these examples (personal communication, June 10, 2002).

and need to model dialogue. On the other, for the students to learn the other tra-dition and refine their theological reflection, it is important that they be fully engaged in the conversation, and not merely watch others "perform" it.

Second, does the representative of the "other" tradition bring to the table a multiplicity of voices from his tradition, or is that representative implicitly expected to embody, to represent in its totality, the other religion? In a theologi-cal school, the students themselves will bring a multiplicity of Christian voices into the dialogue,[22] but it is critical that the representative of the other tradition be invited and encouraged to represent a multiplicity of voices within the tradi-tion.

Third, is the course structured to help the students develop their learning through conversation, or are they simply expected to imitate the conversation modeled by the teachers, even if it is "far ahead" of the students' conversational learning curve? Faculty who teach such courses need to have gifts for helping students develop facility in dialogue; they need not be accomplished leaders of interfaith dialogue. If the evolution of the learners' conversational skills is not facilitated, this learning experience will fall back into a version of the "banking" model, in which the students are merely expected to imitate or parrot back the conversation of their teachers, without themselves coming to understand and develop the conversation or the process behind it. The goal of such a course, the learning process in this book assumes, is to develop the capacity of the students to engage in and facilitate conversation with other religions.

Fourth, does the course design allow for the students' theological reflection, for the "second conversation" in the learning process: their conversation among Christians as Christians to develop more supple and flexible theological language that enables such interfaith conversations? If so, how is this done with some sen-sitivity to the role and presence of the instructor from the other tradition?

In an ideal world, there would be students from both Christianity and from the other tradition in the course; thus there could be both interfaith and intrafaith conversations as part of the course structure. Lacking the presence of learners from both religions, the course must be designed with care and sensitivity to appropriate roles for the non-Christian instructor.

Finally, is the dialogue excessively polite, so cautious and gentle that it ignores genuine conflicts and thus backs off from genuine engagement?

GTU has had a number of successful dialogue courses, all of them cotaught. In 1988, Professor Surjit Singh, an Indian Christian with knowledge of the Hindu tradition and Professor Herman Waetjen, Professor of New Testament, cotaught "The Gita and the Fourth Gospel." Culturally, Professor Singh was Hindu, and by profession he was Christian; he had a long-standing collegial relationship with Professor Waetjen, so that the two of them were comfortable with each other in facilitating a profound and critical conversation that engaged learners deeply

---

[22] How diverse the Christian voices are will vary considerably from institution to institution, but there will be at the very least some diversity of life experience.

both in the Hindu values of the Gita and in Christian reflection on it in relation to the Gospel of John.[23]

For a number of years, the GTU offered a course called "Jesus the Jew," cotaught by a Jewish studies scholar (also a rabbi) and a New Testament professor. The two instructors were present for all sessions, which they had designed collaboratively. Students studied various New Testament texts in light of Jesus' Jewish practices and his relationships with Jewish leaders and movements of his day. This course had a profound impact on students preparing for ministry, developing in them both an appreciation for the Jewish roots of Christianity and sensitivity to the anti-Jewish biases of traditional Christian readings of the New Testament.

I cotaught a course in 1997 that addressed cultural understandings of sacred texts and how they are honored and practiced. This course was cotaught with the Reverend Heng Sure, an American born in Cleveland who found himself deeply drawn to the study and practice of Chinese Buddhism. He studied for years in a monastery in Taiwan, where, fluent in Chinese, he was ordained and sent by his master back to the United States to help with Buddhist education here. He teaches at the City of Ten Thousand Buddhas in Ukiah, California, a Buddhist university that trains monks and nuns from all over East Asia, and he is director of the Institute of World Religions in Berkeley, which offers courses, lectures, and meditation to a broad range of participants, from young people to graduate students.

Heng Sure is a product of and an advocate for traditional Chinese monastic pedagogy, and he brought some of those teaching and learning techniques to our course. Students learned how Chinese people come to honor and practice texts and to understand and appropriate their meanings. Heng Sure is a gifted storyteller, and he frequently regaled us with tales of his monastic studies. My role in this course was to help students connect what Heng Sure was introducing to their understandings of scripture in their own traditions. They compared Chinese ways of honoring and practicing texts to *lectio divina* and other forms of biblical study and exegesis. Our assignments required both an in-depth engagement with Chinese texts in the Chinese mode and an exploration of how and to what extent what the students were learning might be adapted to engagement with the sacred texts of their particular tradition.

I had known Heng Sure for several years as a doctoral student in our program. Despite our long acquaintance and mutual regard, and despite the fact that I have considerable familiarity with Chinese traditions of learning and interpreting texts, it required a good deal of honest conversation to design the course, set parameters, and clarify the goals we had for the students. Our effort paid off in a successful learning experience for students.

---

[23] Norris Palmer, a student in that class, shared this information with me (personal communication, June 21, 2002).

RESOURCES

The previous section discussed and evaluated some of the most common classroom approaches to teaching other religions in theological schools. This section will briefly discuss a number of commonly used resources.

1. Textbooks

Textbooks were briefly touched upon in the previous section. An important principle of a good text is that it include actual voices of the tradition. Those voices should include primary texts, quotations or tales from adherents, and descriptions of living practices of the religion explained or interpreted in the distinctive terms in which the religion represents itself.[24] For example, *A World Religions Reader* includes a variety of texts from a variety of historical periods and sources for each of the religions it covers.[25] While one might always wish for even more diverse voices, this volume vastly expands what was previously available. It is also important, once again, that there be multiple voices and not a single voice, that the internal diversity of the religion be represented in the text. For instance in *Our Religions*, introduced earlier, each of the authors brings a diversity of voices and issues into his presentation of the religion.[26] What needs to be avoided is an overweighted summary of the tradition in terms familiar to students, but external to the tradition. Some introduction or external characterization is common, but it should be put into conversation with the voices of the religion so that the difference of internal and external viewpoints is made visible. Huston Smith's *Religions of Man* fell into this error. His more recent *The World's Religions* is better, but still does not engage the diversity of voices within traditions as well as some other texts.[27] Smith's writing is wonderfully accessible, but the price of that accessibility is the loss of the diverse voices and perspectives of the traditions. Multiauthored textbooks, although often less accessible to students, have the advantage of offering diverse authorial viewpoints, and thus opening up issues of understanding and interpretation. Arvind Sharma's edited collection *Our Religions* and *World Religions in America,* edited by Jacob Neusner, stand as two examples of such volumes.

Faculty persons should also note the often unstated assumptions underlying the learning goals of the textbook: How does the text represent the process of learning another religion, explicitly or implicitly, and are the goals of the text compatible with the goals of the course? Does the text implicitly implant or reinforce in students' minds some of the dangerous assumptions of the "survey of world religions" that was critiqued above? Faculty can also consult reviews of

[24] Geertz, *Local Knowledge,* 58.

[25] Ian S. Markham, ed., *A World Religions Reader*, 2nd ed. (Malden, Mass.: Blackwell, 2000).

[26] Sharma, *Our Religions.*

[27] Huston Smith, *The Religions of Man* (New York: Harper, 1958); idem, *The World's Religions* (San Francisco: HarperSanFrancisco, 1991).

how textbooks present religions, such as Jeffrey Dippmann's "The Tao of Text-books: Taoism in Introductory World Religion Texts."[28]

2. Primary Texts: Classical and Contemporary

For the purposes of this book, I am defining a *textbook* as a comprehensive introduction to a religion, such as Eric Cheetham's *Fundamentals of Mainstream Buddhism.*[29] A *primary text*, on the other hand, is either a translation of a religious classic or scripture, or a volume on a particular aspect of religious life or practice, such as Thich Nhat Hanh's *Miracle of Mindfulness.*[30] There are a number of slender, readable, and affordable volumes on, say, Buddhist, Daoist, or Hindu topics. Such volumes can be very useful, but some thought needs to be given to the particular location and agenda of the author. If the author is an adherent of another religion (e.g., the Vietnamese Buddhist monk Thich Nhat Hanh), the faculty needs to consider carefully the author's relationship to the broader cumulative tradition of which he is a particular representative. What other balancing voices might be used in conjunction with such a text? Is there a way to put the author's writing in an appropriate context so that students understand his particular location within the vast cumulative tradition?

If the text is a translation of a classical primary text, faculty need to do some checking on how highly the translation is regarded and how faithful a translation it is. There are some commonly assigned translations (such as Stephen Mitchell's *Tao Te Ching*[31]) that are less properly translations (Mitchell does not read Classical Chinese) than recastings of a number of prior translations into more readable and contemporary prose. Christian texts and biblical texts have also been so adapted. Faculty members need to understand the nature, intentions, and backgrounds of a text to determine if it meets the needs of their students. Faculty can be helped in this regard by articles reviewing the resources for teaching a particular religion. In this case, for example, *Teaching Theology and Religion* published an article on Teaching Daoism.[32] If a teacher is using the *Tao Te Ching* to introduce students, in Clifford Geertz's phrase, to "the symbolic forms — words, images, institutions, behaviors, in terms of which, in each place, people actually represented themselves to themselves and to one other,"[33] then Mitchell's rendering may be a poor choice. If, however, the course has introduced some of the distinctive and challenging aspects of Daoism through another resource, then

---

[28] Jeffrey Dippmann, "The Tao of Textbooks: Taoism in Introductory World Religion Texts," *Teaching Theology and Religion* 4, no. 1 (February 2001): 40-54.

[29] Eric Cheetham, *Fundamentals of Mainstream Buddhism* (Boston: Charles E. Tuttle, 1994).

[30] Thich Nhat Hanh, *The Miracle of Mindfulness: An Introduction to the Practice of Meditation*, trans. Mobi Ho (Boston: Beacon Press, 1987).

[31] *Tao Te Ching: A New English Version, with Foreword and Notes,* by Stephen Mitchell (New York: HarperPerennial, 1988).

[32] Russell Kirkland, "Teaching Taoism in the 1990s," *Teaching Theology and Religion* 1, no. 2 (June 1998): 111-19.

[33] Geertz, *Local Knowledge,* 58.

Mitchell's volume might serve as an example of how outsiders adapt and incorporate the language of another tradition.

3. Literature

Many faculty persons have found that using literature (myths, tales, novels) is a particularly apt way to invite learners to enter and explore another religious world. Since we all as humans make sense of our own lives by forming narratives (telling our story), we are able to enter into another narrative and "try on" that world for the duration of our reading. David Tracy has suggested that we can engage religious texts only if we allow ourselves to get caught up in them, become a participant in the reality offered by the text.[34]

Literature is also an effective teaching tool in that, unlike philosophical texts, it depicts characters who respond to events around them in light of their values and wisdom (or lack thereof). Readers identify with the characters and are drawn into interpretation, seeking to "make meaning" of the story along with the characters. They identify with Arjuna's dilemma in the *Baghavad Gita* and wrestle with how the "solution" offered by Krishna (renunciation of the fruits of action) would resolve the dilemma for him.

Readers bring their own experiences to bear on their reading and interpretation of the text. Engaging a narrative thus naturally gives rise to the dialogical cycle of interpretation in which the learner's own world is brought into conversation with the world presented within the narrative. The "stories" offered in the voices of the tradition encounter the story the learner has of her own life; the interaction of these two stories shapes her conversation with the tradition. As the conversation furthers the process of understanding, the learner constructs a more informed and sophisticated story of her tradition to make sense of what she has encountered.

One pedagogical challenge of using literary texts is precisely that they offer a rather full and complex world, with details and aspects that draw the curiosity and attention of the students. For instance, the wonderful Chinese novel *Xiyouji* (Journey to the West) is a profound and comic depiction from sixteenth-century China of a religious pilgrimage. Even in the condensed translation by Arthur Waley, called *Monkey*, it is rich with details and practices of Chinese religious life and parodies of those same practices.[35] I have had considerable success in using this novel in the classroom when I have organized a substantial portion of

---

[34] David Tracy, *The Analogical Imagination: Christian Theology and the Culture of Pluralism* (New York: Crossroad, 1986), chapters 3-5; discussed in Susan M. Simonaitis, "Teaching as Conversation," in *The Scope of our Art: The Vocation of the Theological Teacher,* ed. L. Gregory Jones and Stephanie Paulsell (Grand Rapids: Wm. B. Eerdmans, 2002), 104.

[35] Wu Ch'eng-en, *Monkey*, trans. Arthur Waley (New York: Grove Press, 1958). The Waley condensed translation is a mere 305 pages, as opposed to the excellent full translation in four volumes by Anthony Yü (Chicago: University of Chicago Press, 1977-83), which runs to nearly two thousand pages.

a course around it, so that learners could appreciate its richness. I have frustrated students when I have assigned it simply as "a reading" and have tried to deal with it in just a class or two.

A few literary texts have relatively simple and brief structures, such as fables or parables (although, as we all have experienced, a fable or parable may have a complex nest of meanings). I have had success with *Seven Taoist Masters: A Folk Novel of China*, in part because it is a "manual of Taoist training written in the form of a popular novel."[36] Eva Wong's readable translation and condensation keep the novel focused on Daoist practices and values.

Clare Fischer uses novels in a course on comparative ethics to "immerse students in a narrative take on the ethical dilemma set with the corpus of the narrative." The novels make the ethical dilemmas and principles less abstract, portraying them within the rich textures of human experience. This keeps students from too quickly identifying with dilemmas from another tradition; they see in the novels how problems similar to ones they had known are structured very differently in a different setting. Novels such as Barbara Kingsolver's *Poisonwood Bible* (African colonial period) and Naguib Mahfouz's *Journey of Ibn Fattouma* (Islamic)[37] draw students deeply into a conversation between their worlds of values and those depicted in the texts.[38]

Literature offers a rich depiction of a world that—although it enhances and deepens the learners' entry into another world—requires time and attention for an appropriate reading and interpretation.

4. Film and Video

Film and video offer the advantages of a narrative structure to engage students in interpretation and understanding and provide an additional level of immediacy (the students actually see the context and action rather than imagining it). Generally speaking, film and video, because they move at their own pace, draw the viewer through the plot at the pace and in the way that the director intends (unless, of course, the student is watching on the Internet or in other circumstances in which he can pause, rewind, freeze, and review at will). The possibly distracting background details go by very quickly; this can be an advantage. On the other hand, if the teacher wants learners to linger on a particular moment in the film in which religious values or practices are highlighted, she will have to find some way to highlight that moment.

One has to consider the agenda and perspective of the director when choosing a film or video. Does the director represent actual views and voices of the religion or only an outsider's view? Does he offer one particular and contended view

---

[36] "Introduction," in *Seven Taoist Masters: A Folk Novel of China,* trans. Eva Wong (Boston: Shambhala, 1990).

[37] Barbara Kingsolver, *The Poisonwood Bible* (New York: HarperFlamingo, 1999); Naguib Mahfouz, *The Journey of Ibn Fattouma* (New York: Doubleday, 1993).

[38] Clare Fischer, personal communication, June 25, 2002.

of the tradition? If so, that needs to be made clear to the students. Does he represent a view from outside? If so, with what background and purpose? If the location and intentions of the director are identified, then the film can be placed in its proper context and supplemented by other voices and views.

5. Site Visits

Given the religious pluralism of twenty-first-century America, most theological schools are within accessible distance of temples, synagogues, or mosques of other religions. Site visits are an increasingly popular and effective way to give students a firsthand experience of the living presence and concrete reality of other religions.

There are a few caveats, however. In some smaller or more religiously homogeneous towns and cities, some religious sites have been overwhelmed by requests for visits from outsiders. Many are quite gracious about it, but this is in part because they feel that they have to interpret themselves to the broader society in order to win their good will.

Theological schools and their faculty need to develop careful and thoughtful relations to ensure that they, as representatives of a majority culture, are not making unreasonable demands on their neighbors. They need to check in advance for permission to visit and be doubly sure that the arrangements are convenient and not an undue burden on people at the site. They need to listen to the representatives of the religious site to clarify expectations. Theological faculty need to be sure they understand whether the activities they propose for their students at the temple are culturally and religiously appropriate to the site; whether there are cultural or other codes of deportment that visitors should observe. Faculty or facilitators must be certain that their students understand the expectations, the codes of deportment, and appropriate activities at the site and are willing to behave appropriately. Finally, and most important, they need to ensure that a visit to the site is structured and conducted as much as possible on the terms of the site, since it is, after all, the turf of that religious community. These general principles will be best observed if some responsible party from the school has taken the time to establish a solid relationship with an appropriate party at the religious site and to learn and understand the appropriate parameters for a visit.

Another question we need to ask about site visits is what weight they are able to carry in a course. A single visit offers a vivid experience engaging all of the learners' senses. It also has the advantage of both literally and figuratively moving learners onto another ground, having them enter another world. Even the most vivid film or narrative is distanced by the fact that learners engage it through the familiar media of film or printed text. "Reading" a temple or mosque or ritual firsthand requires engagement in a vividly new context; the newness generally heightens the learners' observations of the experience. These are all advantages. On the other hand, a single site visit does not allow learners time to explore the new environment, to begin to appreciate its patterns and structures of meaning. This can be mitigated by careful preparation, by providing learners with a good sense of the context prior to their visit. As Maxine Greene has noted,

> Without some knowledge of connective details, it is extraordinarily diffi-
> cult to overcome abstraction in dealing with other people. A fearful over-
> simplification takes over. . . . We are likely to chart things in terms of
> good/bad, white/black, either/or. We become pawns in a Manichaean alle-
> gory of good and evil.[39]

Prior preparation can give learners frameworks for noticing and beginning to process the connective details.[40]

Even with good preparation, understanding through "being there" requires time and cumulative experience, learning through the trial and error of observation. Even a multiple-visit field experience has its limitations. Instructors need to be aware of what they may reasonably expect of learners within the limits of the learning experience. They may have to supplement the site visit with other forms of learning to help maximize the learners' benefits from on-site learning.

Philip Wickeri reported a particularly successful site visit in his course on Christian witness and interfaith dialogue. He took the class to a two-day retreat at the City of Ten Thousand Buddhas, a Chinese Buddhist monastery and university in Ukiah, California. The two-day visit gave the students an opportunity for a somewhat extended exposure to a range of Buddhist voices, from very rigid and narrow to more embracing. Students were surprised that the Buddhists wanted to know what the Christians believed and why; they had gone thinking that they would ask those questions of the Buddhists. The visit deepened not only the students' appreciation of Buddhism but also their understanding that "there were certain things we had to become clearer about as Christians in order to relate to other religions."[41]

6. Visiting Adherents

An important and commonly used resource for courses is a visiting lecturer or guest from the religion being studied. This is an important resource, since such a guest brings an authentic voice and presents a living example of the religion students are learning. There are, however, a few caveats involved. First, the faculty member should know something about the person invited, either directly or through a reliable source. Some persons are marvelous interpreters and exem-

---

[39] Maxine Greene, *Releasing the Imagination: Essays on Education, the Arts, and Social Change* (San Francisco: Jossey-Bass, 1995), 95.

[40] Norrie Palmer reminds me that the preparation needs to be done carefully so as not to program students into noticing only what the teacher has prepared them for. A good way to counter this danger is to ask students, as part of their assignment, to report on something they noticed that they had not expected to see or hear (personal communication, June 21, 2002).

[41] Philip Wickeri, personal communication, June 10, 2002.

plars of their tradition to adherents of their own community, but very poor at interpreting it to outsiders. Both the students and the guest can have quite a negative experience if this proves to be the case. We noted above Kathryn Campbell's unfortunate example of a Muslim speaker who alienated his audience by responding to a question about amputation of a hand as a punishment for theft with "Why worry about people like that?" The students shut down and pulled back from conversation with him. In another course on Islam, she invited a soft-spoken Muslim couple who undercut many stereotypes. She describes a riveting moment:

> One of the locals interrupted the man's representation, jutted out his jaw and said, "So, do you think Osama bin Ladin will rot in hell?" The speaker looked down pensively, nodded, and said quietly, "Yes. Yes, I think so."[42]

The Muslim speaker understood what prompted the emotionally laden question from his audience and responded not to the question's implicit antipathy to Islam, but rather to the questioner's desire to know whether a Muslim would morally condemn the terrorist acts of bin Ladin.

Second, faculty members need to be clear with guests about the expectations and purpose of their visits. Not only is it advisable to provide visitors with information about the course or unit and what the students will have learned up to that point; it is also wise to give them some parameters for their remarks or their presentations. In turn, students should be informed in advance of the credentials and background of the visitor and the specific purpose for which she is being invited to the class. It might be useful to think with the students ahead of time about questions to be asked or issues to be discussed, to ensure that everyone has compatible expectations.

A visiting speaker is, first and foremost, a guest and thus needs to be treated by faculty and students according to the best codes of hospitality. Such a guest should feel welcome to speak from his particular location and experience, and not be asked or expected to represent his entire tradition.

HOW MIGHT WE LEARN
OTHER RELIGIONS DIFFERENTLY?

Although it is true, and not necessarily a bad thing, that teaching practices, curricular structures, and course structures evolve very slowly—constrained by patterns of human habit, institutional pressures and expectations, the interconnection of all aspects of curriculum, and simple inertia—it is sometimes refreshing to unfetter the imagination, to imagine what teaching and learning might look like if they were not constrained by all the practical considerations and entrenched patterns of behavior.

---

[42] The Reverend Kathryn C. Campbell, personal communication, May 20, 2002.

Included in the following discussion are some examples of innovative approaches to learning other religions that "push the edges" of our thinking; beyond these others can be imagined and implemented.

1. INTERRELIGIOUS LEARNING

Mary Boys and Sara Lee, specialists in religious education from the Roman Catholic and Jewish traditions, respectively, developed an approach to interreligious learning with the help of a grant from the Lilly Foundation. They came to believe that religious educators from their traditions needed a deeper and more vibrant understanding of the other in order to prepare Catholics and Jews to live in a religiously plural world. They were well aware of the history of tensions and misunderstandings that hovered over their two traditions, and they thus needed to offer not just information but face-to-face conversations across religious lines.

Their approach to interreligious learning was to study in the presence of the other, using study to structure an interreligious conversation while encountering the other tradition as embodied in another person.[43] As coleaders, Boys and Lee carefully crafted questions for each section, engaging the learners both cognitively through analysis and affectively by eliciting their personal responses. Although the participants experienced considerable fear and discomfort at the outset and at some stages along the way (they had particular difficulty discussing the Holocaust with one another), the evaluations and responses of the learners showed that the experience was both disquieting and profoundly transforming.[44]

Looking back on their project, they concluded that interreligious learning (1) entails a commitment to an educational process that involves study in the presence of the other, with the two groups of equal size; (2) requires team-teaching with an other whom one trusts; (3) affects many aspects of an individual's religious self-understanding in ways not readily anticipated; (4) provides a way of deepening one's religious commitment while providing a ground for pluralism.[45]

Boys and Lee's interreligious learning project was thoughtfully designed, and the article about it provides helpful evaluations. Seminar participants were carefully selected educators, mature learners already well established as Catholic or Jewish leaders. Because these authors provide excellent description, feedback from participants, and their own evaluation, they offer material from which one might design a course for students. The one challenge for many theological schools is the requirement not only for an interreligious teaching team but also for an interreligious population of students. Some theological schools may be located near an institution of learning or worship that might have students who

---

[43] Mary C. Boys and Sara S. Lee, "The Catholic-Jewish Colloquium: An Experiment in Interreligious Learning," *Religious Education* 91, no. 4 (Fall 1996): 425-35. I thank colleague Kathy Talvacchia for alerting me to this article (personal communication, June 20, 2002).

[44] Ibid., 438-39.

[45] Ibid., 450-56.

would participate in such a course. One can also envision this as a continuing education course, with leaders from two religions in the community participating. The interreligious learning model of Boys and Lee underscores the disadvantages of having too one-sided a classroom (all or almost all Christian students) when seeking to learn another religion.

2. LEARNING OTHER RELIGIONS EXPERIENTIALLY

Jeffrey Carlson developed a fascinating course that applied the model of experiential learning to the study of religious diversity in the city of Chicago, where he teaches at DePaul University. This carefully crafted course engaged students in readings on the issues and then, during an immersion week, assigned a short reading for each site to be visited. Students kept a logbook of hard critical thinking about the issues addressed in the course in terms of what they learned at the various sites.[46] Carlson chose the readings not only to provide context for the sites but also to open up various perspectives of religions. For example, when students visited an African American congregation, they met a pastor with views quite different from those of Cornel West, whose work they had just read. This discrepancy in African American Christian voices stunned the students and challenged them to think more deeply about issues confronting the black church.[47]

The midterm examination in the course allowed students to consult their logbook of reflections but none of the course readings, thus encouraging them to connect their experiential learning to course issues. The second half of the midterm asked them to propose a research project for the second half of the course, delineating the issue and proposing both readings and site visits.[48]

The course also required students to spend one day in community service. The students helped convert a former bar—known for prostitution, drug selling, and gang activity—into an Islamic community center. Not only did they fulfill the requested tasks (pulling weeds, painting); they also spontaneously dismantled and removed the huge ugly electrified sign that had advertised the bar. The gesture was profoundly symbolic and deeply moved the leaders of the Islamic community.[49]

Carlson's well-designed course provides a model for site visits as a means of learning other religions. He explained the experiential learning model to the students so that they would understand the purpose of the site visits. He prepared the students for the site visits and also provided them with some surprises they had to grapple with (differences between the readings and what they heard and saw at the sites). He did not use the sites merely as "resources" (a live textbook,

---

[46] Jeffrey Carlson, "From Site Unseen to Experiential Learning: Religious Studies in the 'Discover Chicago' Model," *Teaching Theology and Religion* 1, no. 2 (June 1998): 120-27.

[47] Ibid., 123-24.

[48] Ibid., 124-25.

[49] Ibid., 125-26.

so to speak), but engaged the students in relationships through community service at the site. The assignments and goals of the course relied heavily on what was learned experientially at the sites, with both the logbook and the exams drawing from the experiential learning. His article is well worth reading by any teacher who proposes to use site visits to enhance understanding.

3. THE SEMINARY ADOPTS A LEARN-ANOTHER-RELIGION PARTNER

One issue frequently raised by articulating the threads of the learning process is how difficult it can be to engage deeply the theological reflection of the students, which is so central to theological education. One way to address this issue, although perhaps a utopian one, is for the theological school to expect everyone, students and faculty, to learn a particular religion and incorporate that ongoing learning, discussion, and reflection across the theological curriculum.

This would begin with a well-designed course (either a semester course, or an intensive course during a January session or other time in which both faculty and students could participate) introducing one religion, with attention to the learning process described in this book: many voices of the tradition represented; a variety of texts, lived experiences, film, and other resources; site visits; structured interreligious conversation and theological reflection; attention to the learning process. The facilitators of this course would also be available to faculty persons to help them design modules dealing with the religion and building on the initial learning experience for their core courses. The facilitators would help faculty to locate readings, speakers, films, and learning experiences that would represent the other religion well and engage significant issues for the core course.

This approach has significant advantages: (1) everyone in the seminary would have a learning base in the tradition, so that conversations and reflections could build on that base; (2) faculty would have informed consultants to help them design effective learning modules that would contribute something to their core courses; (3) the school's learning community would begin to develop ever more supple theological language.

The challenges are also considerable: (1) to find the leadership, time, and school commitment to the common learning experience; (2) to locate course facilitators who can not only lead such a course but also serve as skilled consultants to the faculty; (3) to sustain the experience over a period of years; and (4) to find a suitable way to accommodate the large number of students and faculty in an effective learning experience.

A more limited version of this idea would be to link the course on the other religion to several key courses—the introductions to theology, Bible, and history, for instance, and maybe to ethics as well. Or, alternatively, if the school has a required first-year sequence of courses, the course could be connected to several of those courses. This has the advantage of limiting the number of faculty involved in the project as well as the scope of its ambitions.

4. OTHER IDEAS

Several colleagues who read a draft of this book offered ideas or suggestions for significantly new approaches to learning other religions.

Jim Bretzke suggested that the Internet and technology could be used to design global courses, putting North American students in conversation with students in some other parts of the world. He has put his students in Berkeley in conversations with students in Manila. In this case, all of the students were Roman Catholic. But, in principle, the same technology could be used to establish inter-religious conversations between a seminary in Chicago and a Buddhist university in Taiwan.[50]

Kimberly Whitney suggested organizing a course around a performance or an art exhibit, since art has a way of engaging the imagination and feelings across lines of difference.[51] Several years ago, the Asian Art Museum in San Francisco mounted an extraordinary exhibit on Daoism. A first-rate course on Daoist art and practice could have been structured around that exhibit.

Denis Thalson suggested an exercise that could become a major focus of a course: "trying to re-language some portion of the Christian tradition using the vocabularies and conceptual pantry of another tradition."[52] This is an intriguing notion that would require careful planning. It would be particularly helpful, I believe, in a theology course, where one or two major issues in Christian theology might be "re-languaged" from the standpoint of another tradition, particularly if the course included students from cultures where that tradition was dominant. For instance, Koreans might seek to re-language issues about the Holy Spirit in the language of Daoism, or Japanese might seek to re-language issues of conscience in terms of Confucian "good-knowing." Such an exercise would require faculty with the requisite background, but could deepen theological reflection on two counts: (1) students would explore the possibility of contextualizing some key Christian concepts in Asian cultural terms; and (2) students would probe Christian language more deeply. We tend to use Christian theological language in a conventional way, to repeat what others have said, without ever grappling with the implications of the particular language. Such a re-languaging exercise would force Christians to understand what is at stake in their theological language and to explore it more deeply.

Fumitaka Matsuoka argued for a fundamental shift in thinking. He writes,

I have found that we Christians need to go out of our own familiar setting into a different world in order to really understand what it means to raise different questions and have our own values questioned. Otherwise, our learning will remain an extension of what we already know, rather than a fundamental shift.[53]

---

[50] Personal communication, June 6, 2002.

[51] Personal communication, June 1, 2002.

[52] Personal communication, May 28, 2002.

[53] Personal communication, June 15, 2002.

He proposes that perhaps field education or clinical pastoral education should include sites of religions other than Christianity. This is a fairly radical notion for most theological schools, but if pastors are to be increasingly involved in interfaith activities and interreligious family and marriage counseling, it might be advisable to require some "field" experience in a setting beyond Christianity.

WHERE DO WE GO FROM HERE?

Many faculty will find themselves a bit exhausted (and perhaps discouraged) after reading this chapter. The learning process I have articulated by interweaving ideas from learning theory, the study of religions, and theological learning asks a great deal of both teachers and learners. Like all good critical scholarship on teaching and learning, it brings to light the shortcomings and incoherencies of many of our current practices and seems to suggest or ask for approaches for which we are not yet ready. As we noted at the start of this chapter, teaching practices change very slowly, for both good and not so good reasons. But—to invoke an ancient Chinese proverb—a journey of a thousand miles begins with a single step. The fresh and different proposals discussed in the last section may inspire a new turn at some future time, but in the meantime there are some concrete steps that all faculty can take.

Let us begin by acknowledging the ways in which many seminary faculty members are already moving in the direction advocated by this book. Student diversity in theological schools (in terms of age, gender, ethnic background, sexual orientation, and so forth) has already prompted many theological faculty to adopt pedagogical models like those discussed in this volume—building on students' diverse past experiences to develop conversations that help them articulate their own theological voices and appreciate the diversity of Christian experiences and perspectives within their own denomination. Such pedagogical approaches in all of the theological disciplines help students to understand across boundaries of difference (experiential difference, gender difference, historical difference, cultural difference). Some students may bring to their studies an ethnic or cultural background or a life experience (living in another culture) which has already exposed them to other religions. In such cases, issues of understanding other religions will be an organic part of the development of their Christian self-understandings. Whether or not these issues arise naturally in the lives of students, student-centered, experience-based, and dialogical approaches to teaching will quite naturally address issues of human difference within Christian contexts and will make it easier to address other religions, as these issues might arise in biblical studies, church history, theology, worship, pastoral counseling, or congregational leadership.[54] By extension, the most natural way to address other religions is as they naturally arise out of issues in the course.

---

[54] I thank my colleague Bill Countryman for reminding me of this connection between the pedagogical strategies in my book and those increasingly used by many theological faculty (personal communication, June 11, 2002).

Second, I encourage faculty to seek partnerships with others in their seminaries, in a nearby college or university, or in the community, who can help them to incorporate other religions successfully into their courses, identifying appropriate readings or learning experiences, finding guest speakers or sites to visit, identifying issues that will contribute to the core goals of the course. At GTU we are planning to offer brief seminars or workshops for faculty to develop units or assignments in collaboration with other faculty who can connect them with the appropriate expertise and materials and help them think through the best approaches. They can also be available to help assess what worked or did not work and to improve the unit for the next year's course.

Third, it is advisable to start small: to pick a particular issue, text, or practice of another religion that can be addressed within a seminary course. It is far easier to have students learn Zen Buddhist meditation than to learn all of Buddhism. The teacher can readily identify readings, guest speakers, or a site visit for a specific topic. She can include an experiential learning dimension, and she can identify readings by Christians on Zen Buddhist meditation. Such a unit would fit well into a course on Christian spirituality or prayer.

Fourth, school faculties should discuss at what point in the theological curriculum students would most benefit from learning another religion. Many schools might opt for second or third year, when the student has been grounded in the "basics" of theological education. Others, however, might conclude that some exposure in the first year would open up issues of contemporary Christian identity and community in ways that would enrich other first-year courses. If faculty can decide how such exposure could benefit theological education, it will become clearer at what point, and in what courses, to include learning another religion.

Fifth, awareness of the learning process can be an asset in qualifying a learning experience that is limited or truncated by other demands. The faculty member can help students see how the experience should be fuller, more comprehensive. For example, the class might have compared a Muslim interpretation (or, even better, two Muslim interpretations) of the binding of Isaac with Christian readings, and done some theological reflection on what the contrast has taught them. The professor can remind students that in an ideal world they would have read more Islamic interpretations and engaged in conversations with Muslims about how they wrestle with the meaning of the text. If the focus of the course is to teach methods of biblical interpretation, then the conversations would have helped students learn about Islamic interpretive methods. If the focus of the course is theological or pastoral reflection on the Bible, then the conversations would have deepened their sense of the range of possible readings. By highlighting what more could have been done with a specific exercise in learning another religion, students are encouraged to keep seeking ways of understanding and to find other learning experiences.

Finally, in addition to the human resources and partnerships described above, there are other resources—journals, Web sites, books, and articles—that can help faculty members to consider how best to address these issues. I have included some of these in an annotated bilbiography in Appendix A.

7

Beyond the Classroom

Learning Other Religions in the Churches

Chapter 5 described the threads of the learning process, grounding them in the theoretical issues discussed in chapters 2, 3, and 4. Chapter 6 drew out some of the pedagogical implications, again with reference to learning theories and principles. This chapter builds on the previous discussion as background, but seeks to move as far as possible toward the practical—to provide guidelines and advice for "beyond-the-classroom" learning in the churches.

Parishes or denominational bodies may sponsor retreats, workshops, reading groups, reflection groups, or adult-education forums on the texts, beliefs, or practices of another religion. Parish-sponsored learning experiences seldom provide the sustained, structured learning experience represented in a college or seminary course. These are nonetheless significant learning experiences, and the principles and learning process articulated in this book can help us to think about them *as learning experiences*, so that we will be able to take full advantage of what they offer, understand their limitations, and consider how we might enhance our understanding of other religions and relationships with their adherents.

The chapter will begin with a few models of parish-based or parish-sponsored programs for learning other religions. It will then discuss principles for developing or approaching such programs, suggested by threads of the learning process discussed in chapter 5. In the preface, I suggested that nonacademic readers might want to skip from chapter 1 to chapters 6 and 7, moving from there back to chapter 5, and then to chapters 2 through 4 as those seemed helpful or relevant. In this chapter I will assume that some readers have followed that advice, and therefore I briefly summarize each thread of the learning process in practical terms that might be useful for church-based programs. After each summary, I will explore some of the issues raised for developing parish-based programs. The chapter will conclude with some encouragement for parishes seeking to address these issues.

CHURCH-BASED PROGRAMS
FOR LEARNING OTHER RELIGIONS

There is an astonishing array of programs in parishes helping Christians understand and explore other religions. I have been involved in a good many, in Indiana, California, and Tennessee. For example, I have led a parish weekend retreat on Buddhist spirituality, introducing a variety of spiritual practices and the visual arts associated with them. My parish held a five-week series on Jewish–Christian understanding, which invited guest speakers from local synagogues, as well as the Jewish spouses of several parishioners. We had a special session on Jewish–Christian marriages, focusing both on how the spouses seek to honor the other's tradition, and also on what Christians in those marriages have learned about Jewish–Christian understanding. My parish had a prayer and reflection group during Lent that used Buddhist or Hindu meditation techniques for the first half of the session, discussed responses to them, and then continued in Christian contemplative prayer. I have preached on Daoism in Unitarian Universalist parishes in Indiana and in California. Although the idea of preaching on Daoism was strange to me as an Episcopalian, I have learned a great deal from the experience of casting some of the voices and principles of Daoism in sermon form. I have been a guest speaker in parish-based Wednesday-evening courses on world religions, speaking on Daoism, Confucianism, or Buddhism, the three Asian traditions I know best. I have spoken at Diocesan Conferences and at conferences and workshops sponsored by the Church Divinity School of the Pacific (an Episcopalian seminary at the GTU) for lay persons and alumni of the school on various versions of what I as a Christian have learned from other religions. Such events and programs, I suspect, are familiar to many readers active in adult education in their parishes and denominations.

I would like to highlight two programs designed by colleagues because they provide more unusual and very promising models of what can be done in church-based programs. Together with the more traditional programs I have just described, these will offer multiple examples to be addressed by the learning threads articulated in this book.

The Adult Education Committee of my parish joined with a local Jewish congregation to inaugurate an "evening of conversation" series. The conversations include roughly equal numbers of participants from the Jewish and Christian congregations. The participants meet about once a month (less frequently in the summer, given scheduling difficulties), alternating meetings at the synagogue and at the church. Conversations have begun around religious practices, sharing and explaining practices to one another. They may later proceed to collaborative study and interpretation of religious texts. After the first meetings, the members of the Jewish congregation welcomed any of the Christians in the group to join their ongoing weekly Torah study. The "evenings of conversation" program is a less intensive, more informal version of the "interreligious learning" model developed by Mary Boys and Sara Lee, discussed in chapter 6.[1] The participants in the Boys and Lee colloquium committed to intensive reading and in-depth study of issues in Jewish–Christian relationships. In the "evenings of conversation" program, Christians and Jews are developing mutual understanding through a commitment to a series of conversations over an extended period of time.

The Hazelnut Connection, an ecumenical and interfaith educational resource for spirituality in northeastern Iowa founded by local Episcopal priest Kathryn Campbell, has inaugurated an extraordinary program. Because of the small size of the communities and the local parishes, Campbell decided to establish the Hazelnut Connection independent of any church or denomination, with board members from many denominations and religions. She hoped thereby to attract broad participation and avoid any perception that it was an Episcopalian endeavor. Although the center has a number of programs, those on interfaith learning have been the most effective and enduring.

The most successful offering has been a study group called "Readings in the World Religions," which has met eight or ten times each spring and fall since 1996. The study group is made up mainly of women over fifty with no professional training in religion. These small Iowa communities are still strikingly homogeneous, and have few representatives of other religions or non-European ethnic groups. One Buddhist has lately joined the group to learn more about many religions, but particularly Christianity, to which other members of the group constantly refer. The religiously diverse America described in this book seems a remote reality to these small-town Iowans, something that may be true in the cities, but not in these small communities. "And yet," Campbell writes,

> the people who come faithfully to the World Religions group and do walking meditation and Chinese *qigong* exercises early in the morning during the good weather love learning more about religions very different from their own. They even, after a few years, put what they are learning about other religions into conversation with their own beliefs. And this from quintessentially Middle Americans, mostly well past middle age.[2]

The program's success relies on low-key, respectful, relaxed discussions that start wherever the participants are and on realistic expectations about what and how much people will read. In the beginning, comments were often naive, but the participants' enthusiasm had them bringing in clippings from newspapers and celebrating that they were beginning to understand what was said on the news about other religions and cultures. As they became more informed and practiced, the conversations grew in sophistication.

Although Campbell designed her program to be independent of a parish, the

---

[1] Mary C. Boys and Sara S. Lee, "The Catholic-Jewish Colloquium: An Experiment in Interreligious Learning," *Religious Education* 91, no. 4 (Fall 1996): 421-66.

[2] The Reverend Kathryn Campbell, personal communication, May 20, 2002.

program could be adapted to a parish setting. Such study and reading groups could be short-term, geared to a particular interest. For example, in the wake of September 11, 2001, a parish might decide to learn more about Islam. Or parishioners with relatives who are practicing Buddhism might start a study group about Buddhism. Or, as in Campbell's case, a parish might inaugurate an ongoing study group whose focus would shift as the interests of the members developed.

Thus, parishes can devise a broad range of study groups, programs, conversations, forums, or opportunities for spiritual practice that can engage other religions. The learning process discussed in this book can help leaders think about how best to design these as effective theological learning experiences.

A BALANCING ACT

Theological learning, both in theological schools and in parishes, begins and ends with living religion: that is, it begins with Christians seeking to enhance understanding of Christian tradition and ends with Christians reappropriating that tradition in light of what is learned. When Christians learn other religions, they continue that process of theological learning. Thus, the threads of the learning process articulated in chapter 5 were dominated by two poles: (a) learning the other religion faithfully and (b) reappropriating Christian tradition in light of the learning.

Since many parish-sponsored forums are quite brief in duration, it is easy to slight one or the other of these two poles. Focusing too exclusively on Christian responses and Christian appropriation runs the risk of not learning the other religion faithfully. Focusing entirely on the views or practices of the other religion slights the theological reflection that makes this "Christian" learning. Perhaps the most important principle for Christians learning another religion is to seek to hold these two poles in some kind of balance, in a creative tension.

ENGAGING DIFFERENCE

The first thread of the learning process is *engaging difference:* recognizing and affirming the particularity of the other religion rather than simply approaching it through our own familiar Christian lenses. Engaging difference requires listening carefully to what authentic voices (representatives, rituals, or texts) of living religions tell us, as much as possible in their own terms. Such listening means stretching to learn and understand another religious language—ideas and ways of approaching religion that challenge familiar notions. Such listening also requires letting the representative of the other religion have an equal role in defining the terms and topics of the conversation—not just asking "our" specific questions. Open-ended approaches ("Tell me about being a Buddhist . . .") give the Buddhist more leeway to choose what is important to her than "Do Buddhists believe in God"?

Engaging difference also entails recognizing the differences and complexities within other religions—any single person, text, or temple provides only a small, particularized glimpse of a vast cumulative tradition.[3] When we remember that we always encounter one particular segment of a vast tradition, we will not ask the person, text, or temple we encounter to bear too much weight—to represent fully the whole of the tradition. After all, no single Christian parish can represent fully the whole of its denomination (much less of Christianity); the same is true of any specific and located religious community or its leaders. An additional level of complexity within religions is the close interweaving of cultural and religious practices. When we study Japanese Zen Buddhism, for instance, what is Japanese, and what is Zen? Understanding that distinction provides some basis for seeing, for example, the ways in which Zen might adapt to an American setting.

Christians, being religious persons, understand "religion" as a lived reality that shapes and gives meaning to the lives of adherents. They are more interested in what religions mean to people than in a list of facts about the religion. Wilfred Cantwell Smith understands "religion" as "the history of men and women's religious life, and especially of their faith, lived always in a specific context . . . ."[4] Thus, he comments: "The study of religion is the study of persons, as I have long urged; and indeed of human lives at their most intimate, most profound, most primary, most transcendent."[5] Smith reminds us that "lived religion" does not necessarily mean "alive today," but something that shaped the lives and meanings of human beings like ourselves. Thus, we need to engage the voices of the tradition, either in persons or in their texts and religious practices. As Constance Tarasar wrote, "More than *knowledge about* the other, we need *knowledge of* those who are different from us. We need to try to experience, to whatever extent possible, their tradition—their vision and their way of life."[6]

Face-to-face encounters with persons from another tradition challenge the tendency to keep "others" at bay by means of various abstracting strategies: stereotyping, distancing, categorizing, labeling. As Maxine Greene has written, "It seems clear that the more continuous and authentic personal encounters can be, the less likely will it be that categorizing and distancing take place. People are

---

[3] Recall that Wilfred Cantwell Smith used the term "cumulative tradition," discussed in chapter 3, to refer to the broad historical sweep and complexity of a tradition, contrasting it with the particular segment of that tradition which shapes the life of any given person located in space and time.

[4] Wilfred Cantwell Smith, *Towards a World Theology: Faith and the Comparative History of Religion* (Philadelphia: Westminster Press, 1981; Maryknoll, N.Y.: Orbis Books, 1989), 3.

[5] Ibid., 48.

[6] Constance J. Tarasar, "The Minority Problem: Educating for Identity and Openness," in *Religious Pluralism and Religious Education,* ed. Norma H. Thompson (Birmingham, Ala.: Religious Education Press, 1988), 205-6 (italics in original).

less likely to be treated instrumentally, to be made 'other' by those around."[7] In other words, coming to know a person tends to undercut the stereotypes and categories one group may have about another "category" of persons. Kathryn Campbell notes that a soft-spoken Muslim couple invited to a Hazelnut Connection course on Islam effectively undercut stereotypes learners had of Muslims. She writes,

> All the stereotypes of the macho Muslim male went down the drain when the wife plunked their daughter in his arms while she took the floor to say how good it was that Muslim law meant that all the money she made as a physician was hers and all the money he made was hers, too. And this with glee.[8]

Engaging actual persons and their concrete lived experience provides a form of learning that challenges easy and misleading generalizations.

Firsthand experience can break through a strong sense of alienation between two religious groups. Diana Eck writes movingly of taking her evangelical Christian relatives to visit a Hindu temple and sensing their resistance to this alien setting and its many gods until they witnessed the blessing of a baby brought by a Hindu family for its first visit to a temple. Eck writes,

> No ritual could have created a more readily accessible bridge to Hindu life for my family members. They beamed with delight at the blessing of this newborn and felt honored to be witnesses of this event. When the fruits were returned, blessed by Vishnu, they did not hesitate to receive the bananas and apples, which now seemed to link our family and theirs. There were many things they found perplexing and alien as we continued our tour of the temple, but this ritual blessing had established a common ground of humanity that set everything else in perspective.[9]

The ritual of the baby blessing did not erase all sense of alienation and perplexity for Eck's relatives, but it did establish "a sense of the human meaning of Hindu practice." From that common ground, further engagement was possible.

One can learn directly from another person, face-to-face, or by engaging with a text written by an adherent of the tradition, attending to the voice of the text as a sharing of religious meaning. Learning directly from another person or from a text written by an adherent, therefore, has distinct advantages. The one caveat is

---

[7] Maxine Greene, *Releasing the Imagination: Essays on Education, the Arts, and Social Change* (San Francisco: Jossey-Bass, 1995), 155.

[8] The Reverend Kathryn Campbell, personal communication, May 20, 2002.

[9] Diana L. Eck, *A New Religious America: How a 'Christian Country' Has Become the World's Most Religiously Diverse Nation* (San Francisco: HarperSanFrancisco, 2001), 135.

that cited above in the summary of the learning process: any one person or author represents only a particular segment of the vast cumulative tradition of the "religion" to which she adheres. Learning through another person or text gives access to an authentic, lived experience of the tradition and a chance to engage in a specific conversation which can leave abstractions and generalizations behind; on the other hand, any one person or text by an adherent provides an authentic, but nonetheless located, particular, and therefore limited perspective on a vast religious tradition. It is an excellent entrée to learning another religion, but one must be appropriately modest about what one has learned.

INITIALLY RESPONDING
FROM ONE'S OWN LOCATION

The second thread of learning is *responding from one's own location.* This has two aspects. First, Christians learning other religions come to the engagement as Christians. They might be Christians eagerly seeking some wisdom from another tradition, or they might be Christians who bring considerable skepticism about the religion they are encountering, or somewhere in between. Whatever the case, Christianity is, to some degree or other, their "default" lens for viewing "religion. " Moreover, in parish-based programs, the representatives of the other religion will expect the learners' initial response to be a Christian response. Clarity about the learners' background and distinct location provides a framework for the learning conversation.

What is too often the case, particularly in the brief workshop or forum in a parish, is that the response from the Christians' location is the only and final response of the learning process; instead of providing a framework for conversation, it cuts it short. The response may be overly negative: Buddhists don't believe in God, but that's absurd! Or it may be overly positive: Buddha is the Buddhist equivalent of God. Both responses are understandable as initial reactions from a Christian location, but both contain serious misunderstandings of Buddhism that should be corrected by ongoing conversation with texts, a Buddhist, or a good teacher. As the misperceptions are cleared away, a conversation exploring the deeper convergences and divergences of Buddhist and Christian can come to light. The tendency for learners to get stuck in their initial response from their location tends to argue strongly for multisessioned programs. More than one sessions creates time and space for voicing initial reactions and moving beyond them.

Second, the initial response from the learners' faith locations can give voice to discomforts or fears about engaging another religion. These fears may be fueled by stereotypes we all have of other religions. The learner may believe he has only a tenuous hold on his Christianity, which will fall apart in the face of other beliefs and practices. He may fear conversion or being somehow tainted by the other religion, or he may simply fear the unknown. A program needs to provide a safe space for voicing these fears and for helping participants understand the nature and goals of the learning experience—why and how it is a Christian learning experience. Once again, this argues for multisessioned programs.

Third, recognition about the distinct location from which the Christian approaches the learning encounter also entails honest and appropriate humility. Just as the representative of the other tradition represents only a small and particular segment of the cumulative tradition of his religion, so the Christian learner represents a distinctive, particular, and limited segment of "Christianity." This means that in conversation she is not speaking "for Christianity," but rather from her particular experience of and location within the Christian tradition. It also means that learning the other religion might also help her rediscover an aspect of Christianity. A Hindu colleague who teaches Hinduism at a small heavily Lutheran college in Minnesota found that many of his students were drawn to the mystical traditions in Hinduism as something new, "lacking" in Christianity. He began to include material on Christian mysticism in his courses to alert the students to the mystical strands of their own tradition. It was thus through study of Hinduism (and from a Hindu professor) that students rediscovered the mystical traditions within Christianity.

CONVERSATION WITH THE VOICES OF THE OTHER RELIGION AND AMONG CHRISTIANS

The third learning thread is *conversation,* the mutual give-and-take between the Christian and voices of the other religion. It is a critical conversation in which both resonances and differences are honestly and respectfully explored. A major aspect of Christians learning other religions is mastering this art of interreligious conversation; however, this conversation also entails theological reflection on the part of the Christian. To put it plainly, the Christian's self-understanding is broadened and deepened by learning another religion; she understands Christianity in relationship to broader religious possibilities, perceiving both resonances between Christianity and other religions and points of distinction and difference.

Virtually all of the learning theorists discussed in this book stress conversation and dialogue as an effective (arguably the only effective) mode of learning. Conversation also was the key and most complex thread of the learning process articulated in chapter 5. Parish-based learning also relies heavily on conversation.

Gavin Flood argues that meeting the religious stranger draws one into—even demands—further interaction. He writes, "When I meet the religious stranger, that meeting demands my taking her as a social agent, capable of language and interaction. It demands interaction, and assumes that the realm of our meeting is language. . . ."[10] To meet the other is to be drawn into conversation. Flood argues for a conversation or dialogue that is more than a simple interaction, one that is

---

[10] Gavin Flood, *Beyond Phenomenology: Rethinking the Study of Religion* (London: Cassell, 1999), 218.

a "critical conversation—or even an argument," a conversation that, while mutually respectful, fully engages the differences and disagreements of the two perspectives.[11]

Sometimes theorists can make conversation and dialogue seem beyond the reach of ordinary learners. It is true that the philosophical theory of understanding has provided us with subtle and demanding articulations of how conversation leads to understanding, but educational theorists like Kenneth Bruffee have performed an important service by building on these theories to show how ordinary learners can learn through conversation.[12]

Likewise "dialogue" has too often been seen as the purview of a few specialists, designated by their denominations to represent their religions at church meetings intended to promote religious unity, or scholars engaged in dialogue at academic conferences. Today, however, the situation has changed, for dialogue is happening "on the ground" in a variety of ways. Diana Eck writes,

> [D]ialogue today is not a roundtable or conference that scholars "promote," the implication being that if they did not promote it, it would not happen. Dialogue is already happening, under its own steam, in a multitude of ways, all over the world. And it will go on happening whether or not scholars study it, participate in it, or take no note of it at all.[13]

Eck comments, "The people in our neighborhoods are often ahead of the religious leadership in desiring practical opportunities for dialogue and understanding of their neighbors' faith and world religions."[14] Dialogue and conversation are excellent means of informal, parish-based learning.

The discussion in chapter 5, however, highlights the many aspects of conversations that lead to mutual understanding and learning. Informal conversations can often begin and end with social niceties, finding some rituals of mutual greeting that express courtesy but do not develop understanding. Genuine dialogue requires both parties to listen carefully to the terms of the other, to respond honestly, to be open to correction of misperceptions, and to be willing to explore differences as well as points of resonance or agreement. It is wise to proceed, as we tend to do instinctively in developing a social friendship, from the relatively accessible points of common interest and to put off more difficult points until the relationship is well established. Christians, especially Protestants, have a tendency to ask at the outset, "What do you believe?" Such an approach runs up against major theological differences early on and can inhibit the development of dialogue. It can also dampen conversation with adherents of traditions where the

---

[11] Ibid., 8.

[12] See discussion of Bruffee in chapter 2 above.

[13] Diana L. Eck, "Dialogue and Method: Reconstructing the Study of Religion," in *A Magic Still Dwells: Comparative Religion in the Postmodern Age*, ed. Kimberley C. Patton and Benjamin C. Ray, (Berkeley: University of California Press, 2000), 141.

[14] Eck, *New Religious America*, 135.

primary emphasis is on what an adherent does, for example, Confucianism and Judaism. Thus, my parish and the local synagogue were wise to begin its program of Jewish–Christian conversation with issues of practice. Part of the art of conversation is finding those points of contact from which mutual understanding can be gradually built.

A cultural caveat about conversation may be useful. Persons from other religions and cultural backgrounds may have notions of what is appropriate in conversation and how conversations ought to develop that differ from the assumptions of North Americans. For instance, in East Asia I discovered that older women would ask me questions about my weight or my virginity (items that I considered private); however, they would feel shy about speaking about their religious beliefs, which they considered private. Many Native American communities believe that one must listen and observe a very long time before asking questions or offering a comment; and several traditions hold that certain beliefs and practices may be shared only with someone who has come to merit the knowledge through an extended period of preparation. Moreover, even one's motivation for exploring another religion may be suspect, given Christianity's often triumphalist history. Allowing our partners to shape the topics, directions, and pace of the conversation is both courteous and key to a successful conversation across religious difference. Listening to the other well also means observing signals and signs about what sort of conversation is possible at any given point in a relationship. Moreover, we may learn as much from the ways in which others approach conversations (the forms it takes, how it proceeds) as we do from the content, or perhaps more.[15]

While face-to-face conversation with a person is an excellent entrée to learning another religion, with all the advantages discussed above, it is very seldom the case that face-to-face conversation can carry the entire learning process, for the times we can spend with our conversation partner are too brief to allow for the ongoing in-depth conversation that would lead to mutual understanding. When learners are eager to understand, face-to-face conversation is often supplemented by reading.

Reading, it must be emphasized, does not derail the conversational approach to learning, because the reading and interpretation of texts are themselves dialogical processes.[16] The reader is engaged in a dialogue with the texts, and the dialogue with the texts also helps the reader learn the distinctive language of the other tradition so that she can engage more deeply in mutual conversations with texts or persons. Readings supplement and deepen what is gained in face-to-face conversations. Readings can extend the learning conversation beyond a single session or a weekend retreat in a parish.

Readings, if well chosen, can provide a broader view of the cumulative tradi-

---

[15] Norrie Palmer reports that this was his experience in the Hindu temple and cultural center in which he did his dissertation research. The form and dynamic of a conversation were often more revealing than what was said (personal communication, June 21, 2002).

[16] See discussion of learning threads 1 and 3 in chapter 5.

tion and can remove from the conversation partner some of the burden of carrying the entire tradition. Choosing good readings, as noted in the last chapter, is not easy. It is helpful to get recommendations from a knowledgeable person, to check carefully the author's credentials, and to learn something about the press that publishes the book and the range of its titles. In addition, remember the rather ironic rule of thumb stated in chapter 5: if the book is too readable and accessible, if the language and ideas of the book do not stretch or challenge the reader's familiar assumptions, then the book probably does not represent its distinctive tradition very well.

Reading challenging books, and particularly the translated primary texts of another tradition, can be rough going. However, a reading or study group is a good place to wrestle with texts. Such discussion sessions would function something like Kenneth Bruffee's collaborative learning groups.[17] The exchanges would clarify questions and confusion and seek ways to get answers. Answers may be sought from a conversation partner from the religion studied, from further reading, from a course (brief or longer), or—especially in these times—from the Internet. Another valuable resource is educational television, which frequently offers excellent programs on other religions and cultures. The positive point is that the conversations lead to the desire to continue the learning process in some form. The caution, as always, is that the additional sources to which learners turn need to be carefully evaluated.

Christian learners are used to studying challenging texts, for certainly the Bible poses multiple challenges to readers. Many of the methods used for Bible study could be adapted to the study of other religious texts, particularly primary texts. The one extension of the task in studying and interpreting other religious texts would be to answer the following two questions: (1) How does this text help us understand the other religion faithfully? And (2) what issues does this text raise for Christian theological reflection?

Parishes might encourage members whose lives or interests have engaged them with another religion to form groups to read a text from the religion, seek to understand it, and engage in theological reflection. When motivated by real-life engagement, even such small, informal learning groups can be valuable resources for learning another religion. The drawback is that the learning will be limited by the pooled knowledge of the group. The members will need to continually seek further knowledge and resources.

LIVING OUT WHAT IS LEARNED

The fourth thread of learning is ***living out what is learned*** by developing new relationships or new patterns of thought or forms of action. If learning is about understanding, it is also about establishing Christian relations with religious others, and with the world, on the basis of such deepened understanding.

---

[17] See discussion of Kenneth Bruffee in chapter 2.

Serious conversation and dialogue lead to understanding across lines of difference. Kenneth Bruffee speaks eloquently of learners transcending their local communities "closed by walls of words" to enter into relationships with broader communities by engaging in conversations across the boundaries of communities. When fluency is gained, learners can negotiate a broader range of communities and a broader range of relationships.[18] If learning for understanding creates new relationships, theological learning seeks to fold those new relationships into the Christian life. Theological learning, as we saw in chapter 4, can be seen as the development of wisdom, or of a *habitus*, a set of dispositions and attitudes that shape the Christian life, both collective and individual.[19] Let us briefly examine, then, what sorts of relationships come from learning another religion, and how they relate to Christian wisdom and *habitus*.

First and foremost, learning another religion establishes a base for ongoing relationships not only with the persons one encounters during this study but also with other adherents of the religion one may meet in other settings. These relationships may be warm or extremely cautious, depending on the historical and contemporary tensions between the communities. Native Americans, for instance, may be cautious about others seeking to learn their religions, since there has been a long history of tension and wrongful appropriation. The Christian learning such religions will have increased understanding not only of the traditions and practices but also of the reasons for the caution on the part of Native Americans. In such a case, deeper learning may motivate Christians to back off and be more respectful of Native American views on the matter.

Second, learning may lead to collaboration or cooperation across religious lines. This could take the form of involvement in interfaith community initiatives on youth issues or ecology. Or it might entail sharing worship space with another religious community. I know of several parishes that share space with Jewish congregations. In learning to negotiate sensitive issues about sacred symbols and the configuration of space, the two congregations increase their mutual understanding. In one case that I know of, the two congregations are considering further cooperation in the areas of child care and community service.

Third, learning could lead to mutual visitations during holidays or worship services—particularly, but not exclusively, for the youth of the congregation. Some parishes have participated in Seders with local Jewish congregations or have devised their own Seders with the input of Jewish advisors. Visiting each other's communities for worship and preparing one's guests for what will happen and answering their questions after the visit are fascinating approaches to mutual learning. It is important for Christians to learn to be guests as well as hosts for these events. Christian prominence in the culture and Christian desires to witness to their faith can make gestures of invitation to others seem more like proselyti-

---

[18] See discussion of Kenneth Bruffee in chapter 2. Citation from Kenneth A. Bruffee, *Collaborative Learning: Higher Education, Interdependence, and the Authority of Knowledge*, 2nd ed. (Baltimore: Johns Hopkins University Press, 1999), 3.

[19] See discussions of the nature and goals of theological education in chapter 4.

zation. Willingness to be the guests on the religious turf of another community demonstrates a genuine desire to enter into mutual relationship.

In addition to simply visiting the other, institutions may create interreligious events. A parish in Illinois invited local Korean Christians to celebrate Lunar New Year at the parish. Lunar New Year is the major religious celebration of Korea, with Confucian, Buddhist, and folk elements. The parish sought to welcome the Korean Christians to their community and to learn something of their ancestral traditions.

Fourth, learning other religions can provide a foundation for improving one's relationship with non-Christian relatives, bosses, health-care workers, patients, clients, teachers, or friends. In urban areas, at least, many Christians engage regularly with persons of other religions. Learning about their religions and theologically reflecting on the learning can help Christians understand what it would mean to extend Christian love to those neighbors. Such extensions of learning would require considerable reflection on the practical implications of understanding another religion.

Wilfred Cantwell Smith holds that learning another religion should yield "personal understanding" and "knowledge on which to found friendships." For him, humane knowing always entails relationship because people cannot know each other "except in mutuality; in respect, trust, and equality, if not ultimately love."[20] Humane knowing, understanding, is a relationship of friendship, indeed of love in the Christian sense of loving one's neighbors.

Of what does such friendship consist? First, it consists of wanting to know the friend, to understand and respect her as fully as possible. Second, it consists of recognizing that we can not only give to but also learn from our friend, with the "humility that recognizes that one can learn about oneself and about one's own world from other civilizations."[21] Third, it means entering into relationship, being ready "not only to receive the other but to give oneself,"[22] to stand with and be there for the person. This may entail standing alongside them on an issue of justice. For example, Christians across this country have denounced vandalism of synagogues, temples, and mosques and have helped other religious communities recover from such traumas. There is also the case of Elizabeth Jones, a Unitarian Universalist pastor, who befriended leaders of a group seeking to build a Hindu temple in Livermore, California. She worked with her Fellowship and a local interfaith council to "assuage fears and swing public approval" for the temple.[23]

Friendship may also be expressed in a more personal manner. Thousands of Christians across the country offered themselves as escorts for Muslim women after September 11, 2001, to ease their fears of becoming targets of anti-Arab and

---

[20] Smith, *Towards a World Theology,* 74, 77.

[21] Ibid., 77.

[22] Ibid.

[23] Norris Worrell Palmer, "Pluralism and Religious Identity: The Local Construction and Negotiation of Hindu Identity in the Face of Local and Translocal Forces" (Ph.D. diss., Graduate Theological Union, 2002), 154-55.

anti-Muslim sentiment. Diana Eck offers an example of extraordinary interreligious friendship. As a freshman at Guilford College, Najeeba Sayeed, a Muslim born in America, was facing the prospect of the fast of Ramadan as the sole Muslim in an overwhelmingly Christian environment. As she prepared for her pre-dawn meal on the first day of the fast, she was moved to find a dozen Christian girls from the dormitory ready to join her for this meal as a gesture of support. She was both moved and buoyed by their friendship in supporting her observance of her religious tradition.[24] Not all of her friends observed the fast (they might snack or eat during the day), but they honored her observance of it and gave her support by being there with her. Thus, friendship can take many forms, large or small, but it entails mutual respect, an interest in the friend and the friend's welfare, and a willingness to be present with and for the friend.[25]

A cultural caveat may be helpful here. Americans tend to have relatively loose and easy notions of friendship. We believe in nearly instant friendships: that one friendly gesture or meeting can cement a friendship. Many American friendships are more about feelings like good will, intentions, liking, and interests than about actions; and we are loose and informal about reciprocal obligations. In many cultures, friendships are built slowly, are long-lasting, and are cemented by a long series of reciprocal actions and responses such as small gestures of hospitality, kindness, sharing, or gift-giving. Americans need to take care not to seem overly casual when forging friendships across lines of culture and religion; we need to be alert to signals about the structure, meaning, and obligations of friendship in a given setting.

As more and more Christians establish relations of mutual regard with persons of other religions, their understandings of themselves and of Christianity in relation to the world will be enlarged and enriched. Wilfred Cantwell Smith writes of this broader engagement with the world in its religious diversity:

> I do not mean that Christians will cease to be Christian, or Muslims Muslim. What I mean is that Christians will participate, as Christians, in the religious history of humankind; Muslims will participate in it as Muslims, Jews as Jews, Hindus as Hindus, Buddhists as Buddhists. . . . I choose to participate as a Christian in the world process of religious convergence. For, ultimately, the only community there is, the one to which I know that I truly belong, is the community, world-wide and history-long, of humankind.[26]

---

[24] Eck, *New Religious America,* 275-76.

[25] Jacques Derrida has written of the darker side of friendship, the power politics often at work under the surface of such relationships. While I acknowledge this point, I tend to side with W. C. Smith in seeing friendship as an important ideal toward which I aspire in my relationships (Jacques Derrida, *Politics of Friendship*, trans. George Collins [New York: Verso, 1997]). I thank Matthew Farris for calling the Derrida study to my attention (personal communication, June 1, 2002).

[26] Smith, *Towards a World Theology,* 44.

Smith's notion of one community is rich with diversity: the diversity of history and of cultures and religions. He sees each religious community—indeed each religious life—as interacting with this rich diversity of culture and religion. As Christians begin to understand themselves as Christians in relation to other traditions, they will gradually develop a more adequate theological understanding of religious pluralism.

INTERNALIZING THE LEARNING PROCESS

The final thread is *internalizing the learning process* so that the person becomes adept at the art of learning another religion. She is prepared to enter into the next relationship or the next learning experience and to negotiate it with some confidence. This thread is particularly important in parish-based learning, as such learning is more fragmentary and less sustained than formal learning in the classroom. Perhaps the most important aspect of informal learning is that it leads to the recognition of the need for further learning, an openness to that learning, and some sense of how to proceed, either immediately or at some future time.

The learner needs to be on the lookout for reading, learning experiences, and other opportunities to deepen her understanding. Parish leaders can provide suggestions for further reading, information about courses or PBS programs or local workshops pertaining to the topic. They can determine what sorts of interests participants have in further learning. Is there interest in a reading or study group? An experiential group to explore a religious or spiritual practice? A group to visit a religious community or temple? A group to attend a local film, play, or art exhibit relevant to the religion? Parish bulletin boards, Web pages, or newsletters can help identify ongoing learning opportunities.

Learning is not a "been there, done that" sort of endeavor. It is always part of an ongoing process, for there is always more to learn. In some ways, the parish-based learning programs can be clearer about this "always unfinished" aspect of learning. There is a danger that students, when completing a course, think that they have also completed the learning. Nothing could be further from the truth.

ENCOURAGEMENT FOR PARISHES

Christians now live in an increasingly religiously diverse world. Even in relatively homogeneous areas like small-town Iowa, as Kathryn Campbell has shown, there are good Christian folk who are eager to learn religions different from their own. They are inundated with information and images in the media, some of it accurate, much of it misleading or confusing. They are trying to understand their son's Hindu girlfriend, their daughter's Muslim friends, or the values and aspirations of a Buddhist client. Christians can—and some do—seek to understand religions they encounter through individual reading or, say, by taking a class in Hatha Yoga at the local YMCA. These endeavors may provide them with some knowledge, but the knowledge will be unrelated to their lives and practices as Christians.

I had originally planned a section of "learning on one's feet," exploring how an individual Christian could seek to learn another religion. However, the more I read and thought about the issue, the less sanguine I was about that path of learning. Mary Boys and Sara Lee stressed that the only way to overcome the history of stereotypes and misunderstandings is structured study and conversation in the presence of the other.[27] Moreover, the learning process I articulated through my research involves sustained and mutually critical conversations with persons or texts. Learners need not only conversations with the persons and texts of the other religion but also theological conversations with other Christians to reappropriate Christian tradition in light of their learnings. This level of learning cannot be achieved very successfully on one's own. Nor is an individual likely to get good guidance about the best resources for reading or the most informed representatives of the other tradition. Learning on one's own, then, is always challenging and a bit truncated. Finding others to learn with is important.

Moreover, I am interested in this book not only in individuals learning other religions but also in Christians learning other religions so as to develop new directions and possibilities for Christian theological language. Christians in parishes learning other religions and reappropriating Christian tradition in light of those learnings will, very slowly and gradually, pave the way for Christian theological understandings of religious diversity. This learning is important for the Christian communities as well as for the individuals engaged in it.

Most active Christians have ample opportunity for theological reflection in worship, in Bible reading and prayer, in individual reading or reading groups sponsored by the parish, or at retreats, workshops, and forums. The issue raised here is not the opportunity for theological reflection per se, but the opportunity for theological reflection in response to what Christians are learning from another religion. That is harder to come by. However, a parish community can encourage this type of reflection by welcoming such concerns from a member as appropriate and natural, by not seeing issues raised about Christianity's relationship to another religion as strange, inappropriate, or threatening. One member's learning experience can become a theological stimulus for the larger community.

In this increasingly religiously diverse world, it would be helpful if parishes could help persons engaged with other religions find partners for their learning and for theological reflection. Having public forums or workshops on other religions might be one way for persons with such interests to identify and connect with one another, particularly if the forum were advertised as such an opportunity. In other words, such programs serve a larger function than conveying specific content. They help persons within a parish find others who are asking similar questions or pursuing certain kinds of learning.

---

[27] Boys and Lee, "Catholic-Jewish Colloquium," 435ff.

Parish leaders (lay and ordained) can also pick up on interests and concerns of parishioners. When they learn that someone is trying to understand a Muslim client, or that someone's daughter is dating a Hindu, they should treat this not as an individual "problem" but as a learning experience. Who else in the parish knows something of Islam or Hinduism? Could they band together to increase their learning? Could they share their responses and understandings as Christians? Parish leaders will be more adept at this if they themselves understand the process and purpose of Christians learning other religions.

This chapter has discussed some of the issues entailed in developing parish-based programs for learning other religions. The issues raised here are more fully discussed in chapters 5 and 6. Some resources on teaching other religions are provided in Appendix A. Appendix B provides a checklist of questions to be used when planning a program.

Parishes, like theological schools, face many tasks, and their primary educational task is to increase Christians' understanding of the tradition and its implications in their lives. I am certainly not arguing against that task, nor do I underestimate the time and energy it requires. Yet I believe that learning other religions is also related to that task, particularly as Christians are living in a religiously diverse world and are inundated with images and bits of information (or misinformation) about other religions. Christian religious learning, I believe, is best pursued in a Christian setting, so that Christians can not only come to understand other religions but also to reflect on the implications of that understanding for their Christian lives and communities.

The more that Christian communities recognize and welcome Christians learning other religions, the more the fruits of their learning can be theologically digested and incorporated into a reconstructed Christian identity. It is my conviction that conversations in local parishes are an important element in the process of developing a Christian theological understanding of and response to religious diversity.

Appendix A

Selected Annotated Bibliography

Some Resources for
Teaching Other Religions

Virtually all of us who seek to help Christians learn other religions are stretching beyond our comfort zone in one sense or another. Either we are teaching religions we do not know well, or we have little experience in theological teaching and learning. Thus, we all need resources and assistance with our task. I was not surprised, then, that colleagues and friends who read this book in draft form all clamored for an annotated bibliography of further readings and resources to help in planning such programs.

I understand and honor the request but am hesitant for two reasons. First, I do not claim to know even a small portion of the rich resources available. Given my background, I am most aware of resources on Chinese religions and on a certain range of teaching and learning theory. I no longer teach surveys of world religions, so I do not examine all of the textbooks available. Second, such printed resources are quickly out of date, and new ones are appearing all the time. Any bibliography is already outdated by the time it is published. Given these limitations, I will offer here a very limited bibliography, but will concentrate on resources that are being continuously updated and provide a reference work for finding specific information on the various religions. I begin with the more practical resources and move gradually into some suggestions for background reading on teaching and learning issues.

DEVELOPING SYLLABI, LOCATING RESOURCES, AND FILLING IN GAPS IN KNOWLEDGE

Developing a syllabus, unit, or program that stretches beyond one's field of expertise can be intimidating. You may be able to turn to a knowledgeable expert in your vicinity, but if you know of none, there are sources to consult.

Perhaps the most helpful is at www.aarweb.org, under "The Profession," and then under "Teaching." This portion of the American Academy of Religion Web site was developed under the guidance of the AAR's Committee on Teaching and Learning. The Web site includes *on-line syllabi,* which have been submitted by members of the AAR. The syllabi can be searched by subject or by a key word or phrase. The syllabi provide ideas about readings, assignments, learning experiences, and approaches to teaching a host of religions. Since these syllabi were posted by AAR members, other members can use the AAR directory to locate an address if they wish to ask questions about the course. Thus, the syllabi provide links to faculty with experience in teaching the various religions.

The site also includes a section on *film and videos.* This section indicates which of the on-line syllabi include film or videos, thus enabling the researcher to see not only what resources teachers have used but how they have used them. The film and video section also provides links to sites that provide further resources from film and videos.

The AAR Teaching Web site also has information on teaching workshops and other resources and books on issues related to teaching.

Finally, the Web site has links to an on-line version of *Spotlight on Teaching,* which is published in *Religious Studies News,* the newsletter of AAR and the Society of Biblical Literature (SBL). One can view current and past issues on-line if one has an AAR member ID number. I presume that a similar link is available through the SBL Web site. *Spotlight on Teaching* features articles on a host of·issues related to teaching.

In the wake of September 11, 2001, AAR's *Religious Studies News* offered an invaluable article entitled "Resources for Teaching Islam" (*Religious Studies News, AAR edition,* March 2002). It included short essays by five scholars of Islam from five different universities, who collectively introduced twelve books and two films and also discussed how best to help Americans understand Islam. The article also reprinted a list of "Suggested Resources for the Study of Islam" from the *Newsletter of the American Theological Libraries Association.* This newsletter should be available in all seminary libraries. Jack Ammerman and Steven Blackburn of the library of Hartford Seminary compiled the resource list. Hartford has a major program on Muslim-Christian Studies.

One of the hazards of teaching a religion one does not know well is that students will inevitably ask questions that one cannot answer, thus exposing the gaps in one's knowledge. One resource for filling those knowledge gaps (lamentably, always after the question has been asked) is *The Encyclopedia of Religion* in fifteen volumes, with an index in volume 16 (New York: Macmillan, c. 1987). Mircea Eliade was editor-in-chief of this massive project, assisted by a staff of able editors, who in turn recruited from around the globe authors for articles on myriad aspects of many religions. The articles are excellent and informative and provide resources for further reading.

JOURNALS

Religious Education is a key resource for anyone in theological education, whether in seminaries or in the churches. There is a tendency for those of us not directly in the field of religious or Christian education to view it as belonging to professionals in that field, but it contains helpful articles. For example, in chapter 6, I discussed an article from this journal by Mary C. Boys and Sara S. Lee entitled "The Catholic-Jewish Colloquium: An Experiment in Interreligious Learning" (91, no. 4 [Fall 1996]: 421-66). Not only did the article provide a helpful description of the experiment and of the participants' responses, but it also articulated the principles of "interreligious learning," providing a model for other educators to consider.

Roman Catholic faculty members and church leaders should consult *Catholic Education: A Journal of Inquiry and Practice.*

Another excellent resource is *Teaching Theology and Religion*, a journal developed in conjunction with the Wabash Center for Teaching and Learning in Religion and Theology. Relatively new, this journal offers both theoretical articles and more informal "notes from the classroom" on a broad range of issues—many of them relevant to the concerns of this book.

Among the theoretical articles relevant for this book are the following:

Mary C. Boys, "Engaged Pedagogy: Dialogue and Critical Reflection" (2, no. 3 [October 1999]: 129-36), which explores the use of dialogical and critical conversation in teaching.

Stephen H. Webb and William C. Placher, "Teaching Religion Religiously: A Dialogue" (3, no. 2 [June 2000]: 81-87). Their reflections touch on issues of learning goals, institutional identity, student freedom, and faculty self-revelation, as well as their theological understandings of pedagogy.

Frank E. Reynolds, "Teaching Buddhism in the Postmodern University: Understanding, Critique, Evaluation" (4, no. 1 [February 2001]: 6-14). Although Reynolds's article discusses the university setting, many of the issues are also relevant in theological teaching.

A Special Issue on Teaching with Technology (5, no. 1 [February 2002]) reflects deeply on the advantages and disadvantages of using technology in teaching religion and theology.

The journal's informal notes from the classroom (and its reviews of books in education) often provide practical help for teachers. Let me list just a few of particular relevance to readers of the book.

Naomi Southard and Richard Payne, "Teaching the Introduction to Religions: Religious Pluralism in a Post-Colonial World" (1, no. 1 [February 1998]: 51-57). As we discussed in chapter 6, this article provides an alternative to the world religions survey; it is grounded in the religious pluralism of the

United States and addresses issues of "representation" in a world haunted by tensions of the past two centuries.

Russell Kirkland, "Teaching Taoism in the 1990s" (1, no. 2 [June 1998]: 111-19). A scholar of Daoism provides guidance for getting beyond the uninformed approaches to Daoism represented in many textbooks.

Jeffrey Carlson, "Site Unseen to Experiential Learning: Religious Studies in the 'Discover Chicago' Model" (1, no. 2 [June 1998]: 120-27). As discussed in chapter 6, this article provides an experiential-learning approach to understanding other religions and is valuable reading for anyone planning to use site visits as part of an interreligious learning experience.

Keith Knapp, "New Approaches to Teaching Early Confucianism" (2, no. 1 [February 1999]: 45-54). A Chinese scholar offers his reflections on how best to present classical Confucian ideas, rituals, and religiosity.

G. William Barnard, "Meditation and Masks, Drums and Dramas: Experiential Participatory Exercises in the Comparative Religions Classroom" (2, no. 3 [October 1999]: 169-74). Offers examples of ways to engage students effectively in various aspects of other religions.

Deanna A. Thompson, "Teaching What I'm Not: Embodiment, Race, and Theological Conversation in the Classroom" (3, no. 3 [October 2000]: 164-69). Although this article is about teaching "race" issues, the points she raises are worth pondering in relation to "teaching a religion I am not."

Shun-hing Chan, "Western Theory, Indigenous Religions, and Local Material: Enhancing Learning Motivation among Students of Religious Studies in the Asian Context" (4, no. 1 [February 2001]: 32-39). This article addresses how a Chinese teacher has had to adapt learning theory and material to a local context to engage students. It can help all faculty persons think about the role of context in shaping students' interests and motivations.

Jeffrey Dippmann, "The Tao of Textbooks: Taoism in Introductory World Religion Texts" (4, no. 1 [February 2001]: 40-54). This Daoist scholar critiques the (mis)representations of Daoism in introductory textbooks, and helps faculty members think about more effective ways to present this religion.

I have included a rather extensive list of articles from *Teaching Theology and Religion* in the hopes of motivating colleagues to read this very helpful publication.

Professional associations have in recent years addressed emerging issues in teaching and learning, and some of those reflections make their ways into journals. I want to commend to readers a thematic issue of the *Journal of the American Academy of Religion* (65, no. 4 [Fall 1997]) on "Teaching and Learning in

Religion and Theology." The articles grew out of a consultation on the topic. Seven participants from a range of institutions addressed the following questions:

- What do you understand to be the primary goals for teaching and learning in theology and religion in contemporary America?

- How visible do you think your own commitments should be in the classroom? How does this affect your teaching?

- How do you help students connect what they are learning in different classes? What and how does the study of religion and theology contribute to the intellectual discourse in the university, college, or theological school?

- What does the study of theology and religion contribute to society? Is the goal of good citizenship, however defined, still an aspect of teaching and learning in your field?

- How do you teach students with different levels of knowledge, various commitments, and diverse life experiences? (p. 706)

The articles provide thoughtful and provocative answers to all of the questions.

TEXTBOOKS

I have not taught a broad survey course for fifteen years, and in introductions to a single religion I have eschewed the use of textbooks, relying instead on selecting several more focused texts and providing readings of articles and other resources. I admit, therefore, to being a nonpractitioner when it comes to textbooks. However, I am still sent textbooks, and my students who are going out to teach frequently ask me about them. What I offer, therefore, is limited comments on a few texts. My general advice on choosing texts was offered in chapter 6. I will discuss these few examples in chronological order.

The World's Religions, by Huston Smith (San Francisco: HarperSanFrancisco, 1991; updated and revised version of *Religions of Man* [1958]), is eminently readable, and very popular for that reason. As noted in chapter 6, this work does not present as many diverse voices (and contemporary voices) of the religions as would be advisable. Since Smith is the sole author, his voice is dominant, and that tends to weaken the distinctive voices of and from the religions. The book is also dominated by Smith's perennialist assumptions (that all religions are an instance of a perennial truth or religion), and this weakens his attention to the differences and distinctiveness among religions. On the other hand, Smith is attentive to the varieties of practices within religions, although he does not cite a historically broad range of texts. If teachers use this book, they might profitably supplement it with readings or resources on later developments and contemporary voices and practices of the various religions.

Arvind Sharma's edited *Our Religions: The Seven World Religions Introduced by Preeminent Scholars from each Tradition* (San Francisco: HarperSanFrancisco, 1993) benefits from the fact that each of the articles on a religion was written by a scholar and adherent of that religion—an eminent contemporary interpreter and representative of the tradition. The articles are excellent, discussing the broad sweep and variety of the tradition's history and interspersing brief quotations from a range of authors. Each religion's author has perhaps an overly prominent voice in the presentation of his own tradition, but at least the distinctive perspectives of the traditions are presented clearly. The book might be supplemented with brief readings from other contemporary voices, either theological or literary.

World Religions in America: An Introduction, edited by Jacob Neusner (Louisville: Westminster John Knox Press, 1994), is a multiauthored volume for which Neusner recruited first-rate scholars, who provide a brief history and depiction of the beliefs and practices in the United States. The text does not provide readings or primary voices from the tradition and would have to be supplemented with such materials.

The Major Religions: An Introduction with Texts, by T. Patrick Burke (Malden, Mass.: Blackwell Publishers, 1996), offers both an introduction to the religions and selections from primary texts. Unfortunately, it focuses very heavily on the classical or early periods of non-Western religions and cites only texts from those periods. It does not provide adequate information about later forms or developments or contemporary practices, and the range of voices represented is very limited. As a single-author text, it also lacks the depth and nuance that can be offered by specialists, and this weakens the distinctiveness of each of the traditions.

A World Religions Reader, edited by Ian S. Markham (Malden, Mass.: Blackwell Publishers, 2nd ed. 2000) provides a broad range of readings from primary texts of the various religions, republished, with permission, from earlier sources. The texts represent a broad range of religious and literary sources from various periods in history, including relatively recent history. There is an unfortunate dearth of texts by women. This book is a good companion to other textbooks with few primary texts. Teachers should review it to see if the texts presented will work with their own teaching goals.

Spirituality and World Religions: A Comparative Introduction, by George E. Saint-Laurent (Mountain View, Cal.: Mayfield Publishing, 2000), at first looks to be very promising for the theological classroom. It is quite readable and provides some good information, but it is skimpy on the variety and traditions of practices in the religions. For instance, Buddhism skips from Theravada to Zen, with no discussion of broader Buddhist history. Moreover, it assumes that spiritual formation is primarily through scriptures in all traditions, ignoring a host of literary and other genres that have been central to spirituality in Buddhism and Hinduism, for example. If this book is to be used, it should be supplemented with other sources that bring broader and more contemporary voices, and a larger sense of the influential spiritual literature of the traditions.

World Religions Today, by John L. Esposito, Darrell J. Fasching, and Todd Lewis (Oxford: Oxford University Press, 2002), discusses Christianity, Judaism, Islam, Hinduism, Buddhism, and East Asian religions as they respond to challenges of modernity and globalization. Contemporary issues frame the book; the introduction is "Globalization: World Religions in Everyone's Hometown." Each chapter on a religion begins with the encounter with modernity and then circles back to its historical evolution as a base for discussing the engagement with modernity in more depth. The discussions of the religions include a variety of perspectives, grounded in actual historical issues about women, international relations, or national politics. The book does not include readings from primary sources. If used, it might well be supplemented with such readings, or with literature that explores the religious issues in the religions.

FURTHER READINGS
IN THEOLOGICAL TEACHING AND LEARNING

Chapters 2 through 4 discussed a number of ideas and books about teaching and learning in general, and about religion and theology. I chose for those chapters books that I have found valuable, and commend them to my readers. Here I offer just a few more books that are valuable, two on teaching religions and five on theological teaching and learning.

A three-year National Endowment for the Humanities Project assembled a group of scholars from around the country to develop ideas and resources on teaching religions better. Two of the multiply authored volumes from that project might be helpful to readers of this book.

Tracing Common Themes: Comparative Courses in the Study of Religions, edited by John B. Carman and Steven P. Hopkins (Atlanta: Scholars Press, 1991).

Teaching the Introductory Course in Religious Studies: A Sourcebook, edited by Mark Juergensmeyer (Atlanta: Scholars Press, 1991).

There is a vast literature in theological teaching and learning, but I call to my readers' attention five volumes that I value. I list them in chronological order.

Maria Harris, *Teaching and Religious Imagination: An Essay in the Theology of Teaching* (San Francisco: Harper & Row, 1987).

Mary C. Boys, *Educating in the Faith: Maps and Visions* (San Francisco: Harper & Row, 1989).

Mary Elizabeth Mullino Moore, *Teaching from the Heart: Theology and Educational Method* (Harrisburg, Penn.: Trinity Press International, 1998).

Craig Dykstra, *Growing in the Life of Faith: Education and Christian Practice* (Louisville: Geneva Press, 1999).

The Scope of our Art: The Vocation of the Theological Teacher, edited by L. Gregory Jones and Stephanie Paulsell (Grand Rapids: Wm. B. Eerdmans, 2002).

I hope that my readers will avail themselves of the on-line resources, journals, textbooks, references, and readings provided here to develop material that will best fit their own teaching needs.

Appendix B

Practical Guidelines for Parish Learning Experiences

Retreats, workshops, and forums sponsored by parishes, theological schools, or denominations are perhaps the dominant means by which Christians learn other religions. This appendix translates what was said in chapter 7 into a series of practical questions that may be useful to those planning such events. The questions will be organized around the threads of the learning process.

ENGAGING DIFFERENCE

- How does the event bring in the authentic voices of the other religion as a living religion (i.e., through a guest speaker, a film, a text, a site visit)?

- How does it recognize the diversity within the other religion, either by bringing in diverse voices or by setting the voice around which it is organized into some context?

- How will the speaker, text, film, or visit stretch the assumptions of the learners and expose them to the distinctive language and symbols of the other tradition?

- If a speaker or site visit is involved, how has that person been invited to shape the event along topics of importance to his tradition?

- If a Christian with firsthand knowledge of the tradition will design and lead the event, how will she invite participants to their own firsthand experience of tradition (i.e., through film, a visit, etc.)?

RESPONDING FROM ONE'S OWN LOCATION

- Given the distinctive nature of the parish, can the organizers of the event anticipate questions and concerns, points of openness and resistance to the other tradition? Is there some space during the event for these concerns to be aired and considered? Who will facilitate this part of the discussion?

135

- If a representative from another tradition will speak: (a) Does the church audience need advance preparation to take appropriate advantage of the speaker's presence? (b) Does the speaker need any briefing about the audience in the parish?
- Should the church facilitate a discussion by parish participants after the guest speaker has departed, so that they can reflect on their responses?

CONVERSATION

- How has the learning conversation been structured into the event? If this is a forum, will there be adequate time for conversation with the speaker, or about the film or text? If the forum features a film or text, who will lead the conversation to help represent the authentic voices of the other tradition? If understanding is the goal of the event, will time be allocated to conversation leading to understanding rather than "covering content"?
- How has the theological conversation among Christians been structured into the event? If the event is a forum, should there be a second forum, or at least an invitation to continue conversation in some venue? If it is a retreat or workshop, is the theological conversation structured into the schedule?
- Who facilitates conversation representing the authentic voices of the other tradition? Who facilitates the theological conversation?
- Given the limited time frame of parish events, how will the event encourage ongoing learning and suggest resources and strategies for that learning?

LIVING OUT NEW RELATIONSHIPS

- How are the larger purpose and meaning of the learning event framed? Is the event structured in such a way as to lead to new relationships, whether collective or individual?
- Does the event include some affirmation and acknowledgment of friendships and other relationships across lines of religion among the participants? Are such friendships and their meaning in the lives of parishioners welcomed for discussion in the parish?

INTERNALIZING THE PROCESS

- Is the event framed in such a way as to help participants understand it as part of an ongoing process of Christians learning about other religions?
- Do the organizers of the event frame it to help participants become more informed and confident about learning other religions?

Selected Bibliography

Albanese, Catherine L. *America: Religions and Religion.* 2nd ed. Belmont, Calif.: Wadsworth Publishers, 1992.

Ariarajah, S. Wesley. "Christian Minorities Amidst Other Faith Traditions." *Ecumenical Review* 41, no. 1 (January 1989): 20-28.

Asad, Talal. *Anthropology and the Colonial Encounter.* New York: Humanities Press, 1973.

———. *Genealogies of Religion: Discipline and Reasons of Power in Christianity and Islam.* Baltimore: Johns Hopkins University Press, 1993.

Belenky, Mary Field, Blythe Clinchy, Nancy Goldberger, Jill Tarule. *Women's Ways of Knowing: The Development of Self, Voice, and Mind.* New York: Basic Books, 1986.

Berling, Judith A. *A Pilgrim in Chinese Culture: Negotiating Religious Diversity.* Maryknoll, N.Y.: Orbis Books, 1997.

Berthrong, John H. *The Divine Deli: Religious Identity in the North American Mosaic.* Maryknoll, N.Y.: Orbis Books, 1999.

Boys, Mary C. "Engaged Pedagogy: Dialogue and Critical Reflection." *Teaching Theology and Religion* 2, no. 3 (October 1999): 129-36.

———, and Sara S. Lee. "The Catholic-Jewish Colloquium: An Experiment in Interreligious Learning." *Religious Education* 91, no. 4 (Fall 1996): 421-66.

Bretzke, James T. "Cultural Particularity and the Globalisation of Ethics in Light of Inculturation." *Pacifica* 9 (February 1996): 69-86.

Bruffee, Kenneth A. *Collaborative Learning: Higher Education, Interdependence, and the Authority of Knowledge.* 2nd ed. Baltimore: Johns Hopkins University Press, 1999.

Carlson, Jeffrey. "From Site Unseen to Experiential Learning: Religious Studies in the 'Discover Chicago' Model." *Teaching Theology and Religion* 1, no. 2 (June 1998): 120-27.

Chopp, Rebecca S. *Saving Work: Feminist Practices of Theological Education.* Louisville: Westminster John Knox Press, 1995.

Clooney, Francis X., S.J. *Seeing Through Texts: Doing Theology Among the Srivaisnavas of South India.* Albany: State University of New York Press, 1996.

D'Costa, Gavin, ed. *Christian Uniqueness Reconsidered: The Myth of a Pluralistic Theology of Religions.* Maryknoll, N.Y.: Orbis Books, 1995.

Deloria, Vine. *God is Red.* New York: Dell Publishing, 1973.

Dewey, John. *Art As Experience.* New York: Minton, Balch, 1934.

———. *Democracy and Education.* New York: Free Press, 1916.

Dunne, John S. *The Way of All the Earth: Experiments in Truth and Religion.* New York: Macmillan, 1972.

Eck, Diana L. *A New Religious America: How a "Christian Country" Has Become the World's Most Religiously Diverse Nation.* San Francisco: HarperSanFrancisco, 2001.

———. "Dialogue and Method: Reconstructing the Study of Religion." In *A Magic Still Dwells: Comparative Religion in the Postmodern Age,* edited by Kimberley C. Patton and Benjamin C. Ray, 131-149. Berkeley: University of California Press, 2000.

Eliade, Mircea. *The Sacred and the Profane: The Nature of Religion.* Trans. Willard R. Trask. New York: Harcourt, Brace, and World, 1959.

Farley, Edward. *The Fragility of Knowledge: Theological Education in the Church and the University.* Philadelphia: Fortress Press, 1988.

———. *Theologia: The Fragmentation and Unity of Theological Education.* Philadelphia: Fortress Press, 1983.

Fiorenza, Francis Schüssler. "Theological and Religious Studies: The Contest of the Faculties." In *Shifting Boundaries: Contextual Approaches to the Structure of Theological Education,* edited by Barbara G. Wheeler and Edward Farley, 119-50. Louisville: Westminster John Knox Press, 1991.

Flood, Gavin. *Beyond Phenomenology: Rethinking the Study of Religion.* London: Cassell, 1999.

Freire, Paulo. *Pedagogy of the Heart.* New York: Continuum, 2000.

———. *Pedagogy of the Oppressed.* New York: Herder & Herder, 1970.

Gardner, Howard. *Frames of Mind: A Theory of Multiple Intelligences.* New York: Basic Books, 1983.

———. *Intelligence Reframed: Multiple Intelligences for the 21st Century.* New York: Basic Books, 1999.

Geertz, Clifford. *Islam Observed: Religious Development in Morocco and Indonesia.* New Haven: Yale University Press, 1968.

———. *Local Knowledge: Further Essays in Interpretive Anthropology.* 2nd ed. New York: Basic Books, 2000.

Goldberger, Nancy, Jill Tarule, Blythe Clinchy, and Mary Belenkey, eds. *Knowledge, Difference, and Power: Essays Inspired by Women's Ways of Knowing.* New York: Basic Books, 1996.

Greene, Maxine. *Releasing the Imagination: Essays on Education, the Arts, and Social Change.* San Francisco: Jossey-Bass, 1995.

Heim, S. Mark. *Salvations: Truth and Difference in Religion.* Maryknoll, N.Y.: Orbis Books, 1995.

Hick, John. *A Christian Theology of Religions: The Rainbow of Faiths.* Louisville: Westminster John Knox Press, 1995.

———. *An Interpretation of Religion: Human Responses to the Transcendent.* New Haven: Yale University, Press, 1989.

———, and Paul F. Knitter, eds. *The Myth of Christian Uniqueness.* Maryknoll, N.Y.: Orbis Books, 1987.

Herberg, Will. *Protestant, Catholic, Jew: An Essay in American Religious Sociology.* Garden City, N.Y.: Doubleday, 1955.

Holdrege, Barbara A. "What's Beyond the Post? Comparative Analysis as Critical Method." In *A Magic Still Dwells: Comparative Religion in the Postmodern Age,* edited by Kimberley C. Patton and Benjamin C. Ray, 77–91. Berkeley: University of California Press, 2000.

hooks, bell. *Teaching to Transgress: Education as the Practice of Freedom.* New York: Routledge, 1994.

Jones, L. Gregory, and Stephanie Paulsell, eds. *The Scope of Our Art: The Vocation of the Theological Teacher.* Grand Rapids: Wm. B. Eerdmans, 2002.

Kelsey, David H. *Between Athens and Berlin: The Theological Education Debate.* Grand Rapids: Wm. B. Eerdmans, 1993.

———. *To Understand God Truly: What's Theological about a Theological School?* Louisville: Westminster John Knox Press, 1992.

King, Richard. *Orientalism and Religion: Postcolonial Theory, India, and 'The Mystic East.'* London/New York: Routledge, 1999.

Knitter, Paul F. "Beyond a Mono-religious Theological Education." In *Shifting Boundaries: Contextual Approaches to the Structure of Theological Education*, edited by Barbara G. Wheeler and Edward Farley, 151-80. Louisville: Westminster John Knox Press, 1991.

———. *Jesus and the Other Names: Christian Mission and Global Responsibility.* Maryknoll, N.Y.: Orbis Books, 1996.

———. *No Other Name? A Critical Survey of Christian Attitudes Toward the World Religions.* Maryknoll, N.Y.: Orbis Books, 1984.

———. *One Earth: Many Religions? Multifaith Dialogue and Global Responsibility.* Maryknoll, N.Y.: Orbis Books, 1995.

———. "Toward a Liberation Theology of Religions." In *The Myth of Christian Uniqueness,* edited by John Hick and Paul F. Knitter. Maryknoll, N.Y.: Orbis Books, 1987.

Kraemer, Hendrik. *The Christian Message in a Non-Christian World.* New York: Published for the International Missionary Council by Harper, 1938.

Küng, Hans, and Karl-Josef Kuschel, eds. *A Global Ethic: The Declaration of the Parliament of the World's Religions.* New York: Continuum, 1993.

Lee, James Michael. "The Blessings of Religious Pluralism." In *Religious Pluralism and Religious Education*, edited by Norma H. Thompson, 57-126. Birmingham, Ala.: Religious Education Press, 1988.

Moore, Mary Elizabeth Mullino. *Teaching from the Heart: Theology and Educational Method.* 2nd ed. Harrisburg, Penn.: Trinity Press International, 1998.

Müller, Max. *Introduction to the Science of Religion: Four Lectures Delivered at the Royal Institute.* London: Longmans, Green, 1873.

Neihardt, John G. *Black Elk Speaks; Being the Life Story of a Holy Man of the Oglala Sioux as Told through John G. Neihardt.* Lincoln: University of Nebraska Press, 1979.

Otto, Rudolf. *The Idea of the Holy: An Inquiry into the Non-rational Factor in the Idea of the Divine and its Relation to the Rational.* Translated by John W. Harvey. London: Oxford University Press, 1950. Originally published 1923.

Palmer, Norris Worrell. "Pluralism and Religious Identity: The Local Construction and Negotiation of Hindu Identity in the Face of Local and Translocal Forces." Ph.D. dissertation, Graduate Theological Union, 2002.

Patton, Kimberley C., and Benjamin C. Ray, eds.. *A Magic Still Dwells: Comparative Religion in the Postmodern Age.* Berkeley: University of California Press, 2000.

Perry, William G. *Forms of Intellectual and Ethical Development in the College Years.* New York: Holt, Rinehart, & Winston, 1970.

Phan, Peter, ed. *Christianity and the Wider Ecumenism.* New York: Paragon, 1990.

Pinar, William F. *Autobiography, Politics, and Sexuality: Essays in Curriculum Theory, 1972-1992.* New York: Peter Lang, 1994.

Radhakrishnan, Sarvepalli. *East and West in Religion.* London: G. Allen & Unwin, 1933.

Rorty, Richard. *Contingency, Irony, and Solidarity.* Cambridge: Cambridge University Press, 1989.

———. *Philosophy and the Mirror of Nature.* Princeton: Princeton University Press, 1979.

Said, Edward W. *Orientalism.* New York: Vintage Books, 1979.

Sharpe, Eric J. *Comparative Religion: A History.* 2nd ed. Chicago: Open Court Publishing, 1986.

Shockley, Grant S. "Religious Pluralism and Religious Education: A BlackProtestant Perspective." In *Religious Pluralism and Religious Education*, edited by Norma H. Thompson, 138-70, Birmingham, Ala.: Religious Education Press, 1988.

Simonaitis, Susan M. "Teaching as Conversation." In *The Scope of Our Art: The Vocation of the Theological Teacher*, edited by L. Gregory Jones and Stephanie Paulsell, 99-119. Grand Rapids: Wm. B. Eerdmans, 2002.

Smith, Jonathan Z. *Imagining Religion: From Babylon to Jonestown.* Chicago: University of Chicago Press, 1982.

Smith, Wilfred Cantwell. *Towards a World Theology: Faith and the Comparative History of Religion.* Philadelphia: Westminster Press, 1981; Maryknoll, N.Y.: Orbis Books, 1989.

Song, Choan-Seng. *Tell Us Our Names: Story Theology from an Asian Perspective.* Maryknoll, N.Y.: Orbis Books, 1984.

Southard, Naomi, and Richard Payne. "Teaching the Introduction to Religions: Religious Pluralism in a Post-Colonial World." *Teaching Theology and Religion* 1, no. 1 (February 1998): 51-57.

Swidler, Leonard J. *After the Absolute: The Dialogical Future of Religious Reflection.* Minneapolis: Fortress Press, 1990.

Tarasar, Constance J. "The Minority Problem: Educating for Identity and Openness." In *Religious Pluralism and Religious Education*, edited by Norma H. Thompson, 195-210. Birmingham, Ala.: Religious Education Press, 1988.

Taylor, Charles. *Sources of the Self: The Making of Modern Identity.* Cambridge, Mass.: Harvard University Press, 1989.

Thompson, Norma H. "The Challenge of Religious Pluralism." In *Religious Pluralism and Religious Education*, edited by Norma H. Thompson, 7-36. Birmingham, Ala.: Religious Education Press, 1988.

———. *Religious Pluralism and Religious Education.* Birmingham, Ala.: Religious Education Press, 1988.

Tracy, David. *The Analogical Imagination: Christian Theology and the Culture of Pluralism.* New York: Crossroad, 1986.

———. *Dialogue with the Other: The Inter-Religious Dialogue.* Louvain Theological and Pastoral Monographs 1. Grand Rapids: Wm. B. Eerdmans, 1991.

Wheeler, Barbara G., and Edward Farley, eds. *Shifting Boundaries: Contextual Approaches to the Structure of Theological Education.* Louisville: Westminster John Knox Press, 1991.

Wood, Charles M. *Vision and Discernment: An Orientation in Theological Study.* Atlanta: Scholars Press, 1985.

Yearley, Lee H. "New Religious Virtues and the Study of Religion." Fifteenth Annual University Lecture in Religion, Arizona State University, February 10, 1994. http://www.asu.edu/clas/religious_studies/home/1994lec.html.

Index

acculturation: meaning of, 29n. 24. *See also* reacculturation

agency: development of, 24, 33, 47, 63. *See also* empowerment; voice

America: as Christian country, 15

American Academy of Religion: Teaching Web site of, 128

Americans: religious illiteracy of, 15-16

Bakhtin, Mikhail: on consciousness of others, 41-42

Belenky, Mary Field: on women's ways of knowing, 20-22, 47

Berlin model: of theological education, 52. *See also* education; education, theological; learning

Bible: critical historical studies and, 50; as ground of theological learning, 49-50

Boys, Mary, 129; engaged pedagogy of, 60-61, 63, 125; and interreligious learning, 104, 111-12

Bretzke, James: on meaning of "acculturation," 29n. 24

Bruffee, Kenneth: on collaborative learning, 29-33, 47, 120; on engaging other reli-

gions, 46, 121; on issues involved in learning theory, 90-91, 118; on the language of understanding, 72-73, 77, 91; on teaching other religions, 88, 90-91

Buddhism: communities of, in U.S., 10; conversation and, 80; conversion and, 13; diverse voices of, 38, 114; encounters with adherents of, 14, 77-78; essentialization and, 44; evolution of, 37-38; as "other," 5-6; parish-based programs and, 111, 113; participation of outsiders in, 13; site visits and, 102; survey courses and, 85; teaching of, 46, 90, 94, 96, 109, 116, 129; texts and, 98

Campbell, Kathryn: and Hazelnut Connection, 112-13, 115-16

Carlson, Jeffrey: and experiential learning, 105-6

character: development of, 52

Chopp, Rebecca: on reflection in theological education, 60-61, 63

Christian faith: reappro-

priation of, 71, 73-77. *See also* Christian identity; Christians

Christian identity, 61, 71-73; and study of another religion, 88

Christians: understanding selves as Christians, 61, 117, 125

churches: conversation in, 117; guidelines for learning experiences in, 135-36; learning other religions in, 110-26. *See also* education, theological; religions, learning and teaching other

classroom learning, 81-109; diversity in, 61-62; and learning theories, 82; resources for, 127-34. *See also* education; education, theological; learning; religions, learning and teaching other

communications: as factor in globalization, 8. *See also* globalization

Confucianism: encounters with adherents of, 14, 16, 118-19; and immigration to U.S., 7; interfaith experiences with, 122; presentation of ideas of, 130; teaching of, 28, 107

conscienticization: and educational theory of Paulo Freire, 22-24

Imagining the Sacred, Vernon Ruland, S.J.

Muslim-Christian Relations, Ovey N. Mohammed, S.J.

John Paul II and Interreligious Dialogue, Byron L. Sherwin and Harold Kasi-
mow, editors

Transforming Christianity and the World, John B. Cobb, Jr.

The Divine Deli, John H. Berthrong

Experiencing Scripture in World Religions, Harold Coward, editor

The Meeting of Religions and the Trinity, Gavin D'Costa

Subverting Hatred: The Challenge of Nonviolence in Religious Traditions,
Daniel L. Smith-Christopher, editor

Christianity and Buddhism: A Multi-Cultural History of Their Dialogue,
Whalen Lai and Michael von Brück

Islam, Christianity, and the West: A Troubled History, Rollin Armour, Sr.

Many Mansions? Multiple Religious Belonging, Catherine Cornille, editor

No God But God: A Path to Muslim-Christian Dialogue on the Nature of God,
A. Christian van Gorder